NIZHONI:
THE HIGHER
SELF IN
EDUCATION

by Chris Griscom

Library of Congress Cataloging-in-Publication Data

Griscom, Chris, 1942-
  Nizhoni: The Higher Self In Education

  1. Nizhoni: The School For Global Consciousness 2. Light
Institute (Galisteo, NM) 3. Griscom, Chris, 1942- 4. Spiritual
healing. 5. New Age movement.
I. Title
ISBN 0-9623696-0-8

Library of Congress Number 89-80806

Nizhoni School
Route 3, Box 50
Galisteo, NM 87540

Cover Design: Historical Publications
Cover Photograph: Courtesy of Brian Shields
Typography: SciTran
Printed in the United States of America by BookCrafters, Inc.

ACKNOWLEDGEMENTS

Nizhoni: The Higher Self in Education was conceived by a small group of Nizhoni friends who spent countless hours with me discussing and taping the topics which are included in this book.

To Marlies Cajko, Edith Hathaway, Richard Noll, Shana Noll, and Rick Stevens, I give my most profound gratitude and thanks.

Thanks to my Higher Self for bringing me Alex Petofi, who exemplifies what Nizhoni hopes to offer the world!

TABLE OF CONTENTS

DEDICATION

Nizhoni is dedicated to each and all the youth of the world, who might discover themselves and their unique gifts through their commitment to the path of global consciousness!

PROLOGUE

Today's education is an initiation that lasts too long and so becomes stale. The body has long since matured and the hunger to belong has not been met with satisfaction, while the mind, filled with facts, is caught in the futility of finding meaning. Sentenced to mediocrity, we sleep past the dawn—long into the day of our potential. Numbed, we slip into the twilight of our life and, in a thoughtless wink, relinquish it all.

Education has lost its way. Striving to become all things, it has become nothing; merely the *habit* of disassociated, uninvolved modern man. Education has forgotten its purpose, and imbalanced itself on the side of consumerism, with the illusion that more is better, rather than the recognition that a fertile seed will grow into a whole tree. Reams of endless data produce nothing of accomplishment because so many thinkers of today produce only "things."

In a frenzied gluttony of technological consumption, we have severed the mind from the body, and—even worse—we have begun a race without the spirit, which is the only part of us that knows where we are going. Mankind is suffering an acute crisis because it has not been taught to discover itself. Knowledge of the self is, ultimately, the only knowledge of value. Until we know who we are, we cannot activate our true potential, feel ourselves a part of the world, or find full meaning in anything we study or seek.

We have come to the end of a cycle of growth and now stand ready to breach the void of our present mode of existence and land upon new evolutionary territory. We have studied the mind; we have studied the body. Now the third part of the trilogy could lead us home to fulfillment, to a wholeness which has been alluded to only by the great masters, whose consciousness far exceeds even the dreams of our most advanced visionaries. This is the domain of our spirit, the most compelling, if invisible, driving force in our lives.

We have come to be wedged between two conflicting urges. The one is to respond to an ever more demanding standard of social acceptance requiring long internships in educational mills that certify us as adhering to some code of acceptable likeness. The other urge is a fast-increasing hunger to seek answers to the meaning of our lives: the secrets buried in life and death. It is an inexplicable cosmic energy we sense within ourselves and, in special circumstances, witness outside. It is an undefinable feeling which cannot be ignored. It carries an emotional content of hope and inspiration and reminds us of "God."

Unfortunately, as soon as we think of God, the mind goes back into the darkness of religious dogma and we begin to argue the politics of God in the classroom, separation of church and state, one view of God against another, etc. With that, all expansion ends and we are back to limiting our studies to subjects that lend themselves to the safety of the intellect. Yet we know that we are only using 10% of our brain's potential. If there is to be education of any worth, we must go beyond. How can we pretend to teach if we ourselves cannot penetrate beyond the unenlightened 10%? For that small percentage represents only the linear mind, which cannot compute the vast hologram of universal consciousness.

The moment we are triggered into the 11th or 12th% of our potential, something extraordinary happens. Our perception expands so that we actually think, compute, analyze, and create holographically. We experience. We become!

This is the realm of the genius which is buried within us all. We are accessing a level of consciousness we can unflinchingly call "the divine." It belongs to everyone. On this octave we become aware that there is a purposeful stream of events in the universe and that we are a part of this stream. Once we glimpse this, we begin to scan our vocabulary for the words to describe it: spirit, soul, God, the Higher Self, cosmic energy.

Until this all-pervading consciousness (i.e., the soul, the Higher Self) is a part of the research perspective of any discipline, we will never discover the "relativity" or meaning of that discipline. All knowing of any worth is inextricably bound to the existence of the soul and issues forth from that source of all life—without whose awareness we cannot holographically master any quest, intellectual or otherwise. The silent partner of truth has always been the soul. We must now find the way to use it. It is, in fact, eminently practical to our personal and global lives.

INTRODUCTION

We desperately need a new educational system, a global focus toward educating each child to recognize that he or she lives in a global community that holds a place for the gifts and talents of us all. The future has already closed the gap on the ideological viability of separation. Around the world, we must now reshape our educational curricula to reflect our commonality as one family of Humanity. We must now commit ourselves to work purposefully together to meet the challenges handed down to us by those who did not acknowledge that all Humanity comes under the same jurisdiction of cause and effect—that short-term individual gains too often are paid off in long-term ill effects upon the whole. The fact is, we are an interdependent human organism whose survival depends on harmonious communication.

Our children must be taught to view themselves as a part of a global hologram that can access human potential not only from a multinational perspective, but also in a multidimensional arena that encourages and accelerates human evolution. Our magnificent human repertoire is more than physical experiences and intellectual pursuits. We have individual and collective scenarios of an emotional nature which suspend time and space, and interpret our rational world. The quality of future existence depends on the recognition and restructuring of the subtle energetics that envelop the human psyche. The greatest of these energetics is the spiritual body, which brings relevance to all our endeavors.

In the noise and constant idle stimuli of modern life, we have lost touch with the universal source of our very existence. Is it any wonder that life becomes a broken necklace of meaningless vignettes? The most poignant and vibrant of all explorations, the search for the soul, lies buried under the debris of our pitiful mental attempts to categorize the divine into dogmatic religious discipline—so much so that our spiritual nature becomes a topic of history or philosophy rather than an inherent, ongoing experience serving as a passage for the self to and from unlimited knowing, unfaltering purpose, and unconditional love.

Our educational systems do not address the application of the soul to the dynamics of earthly existence because they lack the vocabulary to describe the energetic realities of the unseen world. And yet, that world exists! There are untapped resources within the dimensions of the "soul" waiting to ferry all Humanity across the evolutionary horizon. Our expanded consciousness has choice. It can participate in the universe in ways only the "greats" among us have ever dreamed.

Educational institutions have cut themselves off from exploring Humanity's inner nature because of the political issues inherent in any study of something so long established as the domain of organized religion. Yet, we could explore our spiritual heritage outside its adaptation by man, free from the limitation of conceptualization, as a pure source of energy available for each of us to use as a link to our life's purpose and all thought, action, and beingness which perpetuates our existence.

This book, *Nizhoni: The Higher Self in Education*, is about the application of spiritual truth to the educational process in a way that can revolutionize our view of the quest for knowledge and how we can learn to become enlightened, global beings. Let us be perfectly clear: the missing element in education today is the recognition and practical application of spiritual wisdom as it effects consciousness, the common denominator of the fact that Humanity is essentially spiritual in nature. This inherent, spiritual element relates to octaves of consciousness which open us to the realm of genius.

If the educational process can harness this spiritual component, the wisdom available for mankind to recognize itself within a universal context will catapult our whole species onto an entirely new plane of reality. We need not become bogged down in the mire of externalized ideologies about "God." Instead, we can unlock the divine mysteries within ourselves and let that formless energy enrich us all. Our conscious capacity is limitless. We are multidimensional beings and, as such, we have great stores of relative "knowledge banks" which can facilitate cognition and problem solving for all aspects of our being.

The purpose of this book, Nizhoni, the Higher Self in Education, is to put forth the principles of discovering a practical path to the greatest of all frontiers: the divine self. This unexplored human facet can bring dignity and wholeness back into the classroom by helping every child find a sense of self worth. Through the grace of the Higher Self, children can be taught to gather "knowing" within the self and apply that knowing from a place of joy and true enlightenment. This should be the goal of education.

It is crucial that educational systems acknowledge a child to be a fully developed soul which, because of its universal consciousness, knows the culture it is entering, its parents, friends, even the muck and mess, and chooses all for its own purposes. If we could look at a newborn baby from the eyes of our own spiritual knowing, we would see that this is not "just" a baby. This is a being which has purposefully chosen to come into a human body, or incarnated. All babies being born now know why they come. They know they will not have time to grow up before they must participate. They will have to use the physical body of a child to manifest the wisdom of their souls. We must seek to realize this truth and help them. The cellular component of our body knows of our divine essence. With it, we could erase disease and confusion and embark upon a path of learning that truly has relevance to this planet.

In the past, when young people passed through puberty and attained an adult's body, they counted. They worked to build new frontiers, to stretch out what was available. They were given a place where they belonged. In the material society of today, our young people don't belong. We give them nothing except, "Stay in school until you're done." We keep prolonging the time they are in school because, in truth, we are a little afraid of them. We keep hoping school will open some door that we are not sure exists. Indeed, there is a surplus of over-educated, over-qualified people who cannot find jobs in their fields. We send our youth away, hoping someone else will make sure they fit into society.

Young people cannot wait to fit into our society! We are losing them. We are losing them to drugs, to alienation. We are losing them even to death. They cannot participate because we foolishly never ask them what they know. We don't even know how to ask them the questions. We tell them what we know and what we know is pitifully small. Everywhere around the world we need to begin to look at our children as fully developed soul be-ings. We need new educational techniques to help them to communicate what they know.

Young people have tremendous energy in their auric fields. If we understood how to use this energy, we would change the communication pat-terns of this world. There is an entire cosmic technology that is virtually ignored because of our lack of training to integrate subtle data. Consciousness is not seated only in the physical body and, therefore, is not dependent on such measures as chronological age to determine its quality.

We must begin to understand that all the children being born today are entities of great light who have come to help us through this darkness, this funnel that we are, as a group, passing through. The young people now have less Karma, less contraction than we. They are, then, more available than ever to participate in this world from the perspective of the wisdom of the soul. We must completely reorder our family structure, our social structure, our global structure, to make room for these evolved beings who are—or could be—our teachers.

For the last few years, the ethereal airs have been jammed with entities attempting to get in, attempting to be born exactly for the purpose of participating. It is such an illusion we have that we could in any way protect our teenagers, our young people, from the disasters around us. They have come to help us. What is now necessary is that we find out who we are so we can all, young and old, accelerate the evolutionary leap of consciousness necessary for our species to survive the global changes we ourselves have set into motion.

Nizhoni: The Higher Self in Education is based on the pilot program of the Nizhoni School for Global Consciousness, as well as on a previous summer school I directed for six years in Galisteo. The Nizhoni School for Global Consciousness is designed to allow young people from around the world to live in an environment of their own kind, connected to their Higher Selves. The Higher Self focuses and directs the search for knowledge, piercing the veil of consciousness so the young people can utilize the brilliance available to them— both in their individual lives and in a global context. Throughout this book, we will set forth new, evolutionary approaches to education in the context of the whole self creating an environment in which learning embraces all aspects of our being: physical, mental, emotional, and spiritual.

Our spiritual nature has been left unexplored in the past and it is this human attribute that offers a whole new spectrum of possibilities for the solutions to our present dilemmas, whether they are personal or planetary. The link between spiritual awareness and accelerated intelligence is breathtaking! In this book, we will describe the techniques of consciousness and the curriculum set in motion for our year-round Nizhoni School. We will articulate how education can become a more meaningful experience for young people searching for purpose in their lives. They are the yardstick of tomorrow's world; let it be our purpose to help them!

OUR SPIRITUAL NATURE: THE GIFT OF KNOWING

We have a thought form to which we unconsciously adhere that insists we must struggle, we must search and work and slave to obtain the right to knowledge or capacity in some field. It is only through this effort that we can become successful. We must pay our dues, as it were, within any element of society or career lines in order to emerge as someone who counts. Against the background of this exhaustive struggle, we learn very early in life to weigh the odds, to pit ourselves against friend and enemy on the unlikely chance we will find our way through the maze to some mythical place in the sun. The recognition and the gift Nizhoni has to offer is that, because our potential for consciousness is unlimited, we need not focus on the struggle to understand or to gain knowledge. Instead, the focus is on unlocking and tapping the innate reservoir of knowing within each being, within each of us.

The students at Nizhoni learn to access what it is that inspires them. They know they have within themselves the capacity to successfully become whomever they desire in the world. We, at Nizhoni, take upon ourselves the challenge to see to it that these young people bring their desires full circle through the octaves of manifestation, so that they can actually produce what they envision. To achieve this, we simply have to guide the native intelligence of any being along its own pathway, the pathway of least resistance to fruition of his or her dream. Because it is connected to the soul's desire, the purpose of that person's life unfolds quite naturally. Rather than inanely molding our youth to a stale, preexisting world, let us champion the maturation of a fresh, new species coming into its own. The spontaneous unfolding of its requisite variety is the very matrix of our future. As we pursue each intersecting thread, we enhance our appreciation for the rich perfection of the whole. While we seek further and further to know it all, we discover that exploration itself is more desirable than the goal.

We are here to learn. Nizhoni teaches young people that learning is instinctive, that we needn't resist it. We have the capacity to grasp any subject matter in a profound, holographic way within its own meaning, so that there is never something we are learning that is outside a frame of reference of reality. We begin to learn from our experience. It is the natural state of human nature to be inquisitive, to hunger for knowledge. All we need to do is to access our ability to experience ourselves learning "joyously." Through the technology of consciousness, we can open the gates of knowledge and expand the mind's capacity to absorb new information, to become stimulated and to see, most importantly, the relationship between a piece of data and how it fits in with our personal internal and external reality structures, as well as on a global octave. Thus, every piece of information finds its niche amplifying the integration of the whole.

That is the difference between three generations ago and these generations. Three generations ago we were still aspiring. We still thought there was a place out there in this world where we could count, where we could create something new. This dream is dying all over the world. Young people all over the world are suffering from the sense that they have nothing to give and that nobody wants it, anyway. As a result, they are becoming passive, and the passivity is killing their vital, fresh perspectives, without which we cannot advance or evolve.

The question is not about whether we should teach more math, whether we should have more control, whether we should have a more emotional approach, etc. As educators, we play with alternatives, play with ABC's, but we are not making a *qualitative* change. By the time our children enter school, they have already set up the patterns of how to communicate in the outside world based on the karmic, familial communication system they have learned at home. They make conscious choices. This is why experiencing our spiritual nature even at a tender age can help us to dissolve those crystallizations of what we have already become, and what our fate is in the world. By using spiritual understanding, we can access an expanded reality that allows us to comprehend each person's purpose in life. We must address that purpose. Otherwise, no matter how educated we become, we are depressed. We are not present. We are incapable of giving a gift to life because we don't feel it inside ourselves. We will not think of new ideas. We will not create new technologies that enhance life.

If we can trust the individual and trust what comes through from the Higher Self, then the whole of education becomes a tool in the hand. The test value of any educational system lies in the result, the manifestations, the people, products, and services that issue forth from it. The yardstick is not a test score, but an integration of knowledge that produces something—an answer, insight, poem, technology, fully assimilated and capable of unleashing a very creative, powerful genius. The mark of a world leader is the ability to look out and see everything as a potential tool, not as an obstacle.

What makes it possible for a human being of any age to be more aware of what he or she truly knows? By tabulating intuitive nuances such as sense perceptions and correlating them with "increments of meaning," we arrive at a stillpoint of recognition upon which we can amplify understanding and, therefore, growth. It is simply that the mind is an antenna capable of "associative recognition." This means that we register particles of meaning by association through a cognitive system composed of a multidimensional repertoire that is multibodied and orchestrated by cellular mind, whose components can reach into the past and future to flash the seed of recognition upon the screen of the mind. An example of this is the way children inexplicably comprehend specific understandings of things to which they have had no prior exposure. Infants often will respond with flawless accuracy to communication given them in a foreign language. Subtle gestures, a lilting sound coupled with pace and cadence of a language provide them with universal communication keys, which are referenced in their brain with some timeless data bank providing them enough association to decode meaning.

As we explore these multidimensional avenues of the mind, we will begin to view a vast matrix of intelligence which will provide us with new meaning for complex systems of evolution and "inheritance," by galaxial history maps as well as human DNA! The knowing we have by our very living existence allows us to bring information into our mental computer, to be aware of the complex sets of data that come in constantly on multiple levels of consciousness. This data has to do with survival memory, with creativity, with problem solving, with emotions. This living information is constantly distributed by the brain's meticulous and miraculous computer-like capacities. It issues forth from what we call the "Higher Mind," which can radiate out and access octaves of cognition which are themselves attached holographically to bits and pieces of information that allow us to sum up or to come upon holographic awareness. This is how deep levels of knowing take place. They do not occur in a linear fashion wherein the mind takes in data it has no capacity to assimilate simultaneously with other pieces of data that might bring about an answer or a recognition of truth, but, rather, it tracks and sorts disassociated concepts and thoughts.

Once we can stimulate the mind into higher octaves of cognition, it is then capable of processing or reprocessing data in a holographic manner in which it can supply the question and the answer simultaneously. Thus can we see how everything fits together. This is the mechanism of problem-solving and here exists the special domain of genius, the ability to synthesize. In order for a person to experience oneself as "the knower," no matter what the perspective of the knowing, whether it has to do with emotional, scientific, creative, or problem solving information, s.he must move inside and alter the frequency of the brain into alpha and theta patterns to trigger the higher mind.

Younger people, children below the age of twelve, can access these brain frequencies readily. This is part of why they are faster learners. For example, they can learn languages so easily because they take in the inflection, the unusual associations of interpersonal communication. Their brains are exercising all the time. They are already in deeper brain patterning levels, alpha levels of pulsation, that make it easier to perceive more holographically, rather than through the limitation of the beta frequencies most often experienced by adults. In beta frequencies we can take in data, but we are unable to organize that data synchronistically or synergistically into sets of meaning which give us a comprehensive scan of work.

The trick, initially, is to trigger the brain to alter its patternings so that it functions on the slower alpha brain frequency. Anyone can do this by simply using meditative techniques and awarenesses that help the body move into alpha and theta levels, effectively shutting off the processes of the beta "outer mind." This allows a peaceful expansion wherein the consciousness can "stretch out" and explore because the ego has temporarily let go of its grip on our precarious state of separation and survival. If this blissful silence is allowed to take hold, the two lobes of the brain begin to harmonize with each other and fall naturally into sync. When they pulsate in sync, we can access the higher mind. From this lofty threshold of consciousness, we experience ourselves multidimensionally. Our data repertoire explodes into spiraling streams of associative recognition that fully satisfy our thirst for knowing from every point of the hologram—intellectually, spiritually, emotionally. Joyous, ecstatic learning is Now!

Knowing is not simply a technical exercise, however. Knowing is a spiritual exercise. In other words, it incorporates the wholeness of a human being so that when we have a deep knowing it is very different from an intellectual understanding. We participate in knowings holographically. To do that, we must access our spiritual energy—which is our birthright. We have to penetrate deeper aspects of the brain and delve into its creative, nonlinear aspects, by bringing into the proximity of ourselves, our limited spiritual nature. Our awareness expands itself, radiating out to include higher octaves of consciousness, to become the knower.

Then, if we look at a problem or a person, we can have a perception which sees that person or problem in its entirety, in its multidimensional reality.

If you think of a hologram as a circle that has depth to it, that has many layers, you can understand that if you are only touching one layer, or only focusing on one part of that circle, then you cannot be cognizant of enough data to have knowing. Knowing is all-inclusive. It allows the palpation of consciousness to include spiritual understanding, which demonstrates and sources purpose in any reality.

For example, the workings of the master glands of the body and specialized cells in parts of the brain, allow us to be telepathic. Knowing allows us to be aware of subtle communications among ourselves, between ourselves and other species, and also communications between ourselves and other octaves of consciousness which are not rooted in our time and space modality. This can be valuable to us. This has always been the way the genius octave of mentality and thinking has come about. When we are able to trigger these higher mind capacities, we have a whole volume of data we can assimilate and use to come to the point of clarity which we call "knowing."

Meditation is a technique used in Nizhoni to help us access these expanded reaches of consciousness. By simply triggering certain electromagnetic pulsations in the brain, we alter ourselves in a way that opens the threshold, opens the window to expanded consciousness. Through meditation, we can trigger ourselves into deeper octaves of knowing, more expanded consciousness that allows for cognition on the genius level. We, ourselves, become multidimensional by using our spiritual nature. It is within the capacity of our consciousness to extend itself out into other realms of perception. These capacities of heightened perception realize our human potential.

We now know that heightened awareness happens at deep alpha and theta brain wave levels. These levels access an expansion, a genius octave of unlimited consciousness. They can simply sing out, searching for some specific nuance and bring back an answer or a correlation that is like opening a file in a computer program. It allows us to access information that would normally be unavailable to us in our linear, outer, beta brain patterning. A spiritual octave implies the expansion of consciousness into fast vibrational waves, divine levels without limitation. We are able to avail ourselves of knowing because we are not dealing with the part of ourselves which denies that knowing. Our emotional bodies and our intellectual perceptions very often interfere with the genius octave by saying, "Oh, no, you cannot know that. Where is the proof? This is beyond my capabilities!" The personal ego level limits the ability to perceive holographically.

When we are able to remove those limited octaves of perception, spin them, quicken them, they no longer have a grip on the linear mind, and our intelligence begins to expand. It allows itself to recognize data coming in of a more subtle, holographic perspective. The moment we begin to perceive holographically, we move into octaves of brilliance and become "the knowers." The human being has specific capabilities of functioning on octaves faster than the speed of light. This is how advanced abilities, such as telepathy, take place. It is not just a quirk or a disruption of the brain's patterning. It is an aspect of each person's potential. The educational process has not yet realized the values of these faculties to enhance learning and, in fact, to enrich our lives.

The Nizhoni process opens the threshold to these telepathic perceptions and higher capacities of human nature so that they can be utilized on a day-to-day basis. We are learning to see how valuable it can be to help the brain exercise its potential for telepathy, for gathering data that may be multidimensional in nature, or may have to do with octaves or dimensions of which we are not normally cognizant. We can greatly enhance the brain's informational system by triggering the threshold of consciousness and exercising the faculties for telepathy, etc. These intuitive qualities of the sixth sense are underused and underdeveloped simply because we have not focused our awareness or our attention there. A lingering distrust and superstitious residue has kept them wrapped in the dark cloak of the middle ages. However, there has been more than sufficient scientific study of them in the last 30 years to demonstrate that they are an integral part of human potential, not isolated aberrant capabilities claimed by a few. By focusing the power of the cognitive left brain, which is so good at organizing information, and shining its light onto the great wealth of the creative right brain, we can bring about a synthesis that frees holographic knowing to take place. Every human has this potential!

The pineal and the pituitary glands do function in these ways and provide the mechanism for triggering higher awareness. They are antennas which transmit and receive information at velocities faster than the speed of light. We can through them begin to draw into our consciousness information and perceptions which would otherwise be unavailable to us but which are vital to the process of moving through the evolutionary threshold.

It is time, in our educational system, for us to pay attention to more amplified systems of perception that can expand our problem-solving capacity. This is the computer age, yet the higher mind is the greatest computer in the entire cosmos. It is very important that the educational process come out of the dark ages and begin to apply the knowledge which is now available about how the brain works so that we can greatly facilitate and improve the learning process.

It should be viewed as the educational right of every human being to be trained to access genius levels of knowing. We are, each and every one, the knower. By bringing into awareness the spiritual quality, we can use all these tools of consciousness to become aware of the answers and choices that shape our participation in life. We need to revise our understanding of this element we call "the mind." As we view the potential of the higher mind to gain information by attuning itself to any source of information it needs via collective unconscious, "Hundredth Monkey Effect," we begin to reshape our view of individual consciousness.

Each human being has this potential lying dormant. Because our educational process has not included an understanding of our vast spiritual nature or these higher frequencies of intelligence and actualization, our consciousness has been left relatively idle. By using what we already know about human potential and placing it in its proper place in the classroom, within the educational system, we can begin to develop a new kind of wholeness, a new, whole being who is independent, inner-directed, and capable of profound communication inclusive of intellectual, creative, and spiritual qualities.

The human being can come from deep within the personal self and extend out to the global self. Global consciousness has come of age and Nizhoni has developed the techniques and skills to bring it into focus. We are, each one of us, an instrument of global unfoldment. The brain can be used to 100% of its capacity, rather than the 10% we are, on the average, using now. It must be trained and exercised in holographic consciousness. The brain never resists learning. Cognition is the brain's true purpose. It is easy for the brain to take in data when it is orchestrated to these harmonics of learning.

The antithesis of this is the habit of discoordinated, out-of-sync rhythms of the left and right lobes of the brain. Sadly, we take in the information but do not compose anything new with it. Because we do not synthesize it, we don't expand it so that it can allow the great "Aha!" of enlightened comprehension, so that it can most effectively solve problems. Brain research indicates that synchronization of both lobes results in synthesizing consciousness across the veil and on beyond the 11th percentile.

This is a revolutionary awareness that we can, by creating a more synchronistic environment, allow the brain to take in information and go a step further to assimilate and then design something new, to manifest that information, whether it is an understanding of a technical, mathematical, or scientific reality, or an understanding of how to use holographic awareness to become more creative and fulfilled in life.

As we expose the students to entire spectra of information related to a given subject, they can more easily gravitate to the specific areas towards which they have natural affinity. Because they are not isolated within that area, they more readily devote themselves to in-depth study and, therefore, higher levels of mastery. When people begin to think holographically, they they see the interweaving the interweaving, the interconnectedness of all things, of all information, of all experience. That process takes place through contact with our spiritual nature, our Higher Self. The Higher Self begins to explode the creative process so that the young people take in data that interests them, that fascinates them, and they begin to compose. It is like participating in a chemical chain reaction. The young person is able to recognize what is meaningful to him or her and is able to systematically construct increments of meaning from massive amounts of data which heretofore have simply lain dormant in the sleeping computer disks of a disassociated mind. The student is then able to pluck that meaning and begin to compose and coalesce it into a formidable base of cognition which supports exploration into vast fields of related data, i.e., the spiraling hologram of knowing.

Math, to the student, suddenly is experienced as relevant to other aspects of learning. The student can now see how what s.he is studying applies to daily life, the natural environment, and global understanding. S.he creates a magnificent chain of events by which each new composition, each new coalescence of data, creates a new understanding which expands the consciousness and awareness. It is like a chain reaction of events which allows the person to extract the central core of meaning from extraneous data, and then to manifest something new with that. Instead of isolating specific areas, what we have now is the capacity to understand the interconnectedness of all things: of science and spirit, of spirit and matter, of mind and body. Thus, young people can holographically participate in this world. Each becomes the center point of an integrated world.

All this occurs because there is a spiritual feeding of the student here at Nizhoni. There is a heightened level of excitement because of the element of self discovery, because of the exploration of the inner world as it sounds and feels to a young person, who is normally in such a precarious position during these years. There is a sense of "Going Home" that brings with it adventure and play. These are transcending qualities! Frustration, anger, and depression disappear to be replaced by confident and joyous self-expression.

Exploring ourselves from the position of multidimensionality, viewing all the wondrous parts which compose the whole, are great learning experiences. For instance, music students may enrich their musical repertoire by exploring the history of sound, the history of different instruments and how they exemplify different cultures, and the effect on culture of unique sounds—or culture's effect on sound. What happens when we allow music to bring cultures together? We can look at it politically, historically, and culturally, even scientifically and mathematically. The student, in making the music and focusing his or her attention there, begins to coalesce a profound center of meaning wherein he or she sits in the middle and is able to expand the choices of interaction. History is no longer a flat, dead recitation of dates and events, but achieves a kaleidoscopic fascination. Political science, too, is not a strange world separate from culture, or daily life, but, instead, reflects and personifies it. This is what is very exciting about holographic learning.

Special talents and gifts are tapped, and the whole being rises to do what he or she has been born to do: to interact with life. This exploration by participation prevents burnout. Young people reach the point of burnout when they are unable to express themselves except in one modality. Let us say that they can only function intellectually in a classroom. Their emotions, their spiritual heart, their physical bodies want to interact with the data, but are somehow cordoned off. If we do not provide an environment that allows for that total interaction, there is the burnout. Students become exhausted, holding their energy to one avenue, one funnel. It does not allow them to interact with their world. This is what creates burnout; when we are forced down one pathway and not enough of ourselves is expressed there to feel alive.

Nizhoni provides a magical reorganization, a re-coalescing of information that allows for the building blocks of expanded awareness. These chemical reactions of reality start to impinge upon and spark each other. Accessing our spiritual knowing quickens the learning process. Most importantly, it stretches learning to an experience of intimate relevance and fun. In today's world, where life has deteriorated to passive existence, a new wave of young people who can actively participate may be the only hope of pushing us through this evolution onto a new octave of reality, one capable of shaping the future of the human race.

Nizhoni

and the

Child

Nizhoni is a Navaho word which means "beauty way." It speaks of a sense that everything is in its place—harmonic with everything else. Nizhoni is the perfect state of the child whose Higher Self is still echoing out from that bright and happy face. A child is an unresisting vehicle of the Higher Self who views all the world around as a part of its being. It does not know there is a need to struggle to be heard, seen, or loved. A child's reality can be full of ecstasy and joy and forgiveness because it lives in the ever-expanding present. It does not seek itself in the unrelenting demands of future choices. The Higher Self radiates and whispers and guides the child so that it has the experience of the Nizhoni, "beauty way."

It is only as it comes to be influenced by us, as it must enter into our world, that the child leaves behind the wisdom and the rapture of the Higher Self. When children enter the classroom, it is the final and often abrupt closing of the doors to their unlimited selves. They begin to be taught that they can fail. They begin to be taught how to clone themselves, how to be molded in order to please and to survive.

It is important for parents to know that by the age of seven most of the far-reaching impressions and imprints they would pass to their children have been given. The children will now begin to take on the cloak of Karma, the weight of finding the Self in the world, the world of other selves searching, of people not predisposed to applaud the child for its multidimensionality, for its wonderment.

Instead, they attempt to squeeze from the child any extraneous behavior, ideas, or feelings that do not contribute to a well-disciplined, controlled classroom environment. In so doing, the child becomes numb. The first seeds of inertia have been sown.

It is true that we are beginning to recognize that, by forcing the child too early into the linear left brain, we deprive it of crucial developmental stages. This deprivation reveals itself tragically as more and more children suffer from mental and emotional imbalances in today's world. What we have perceived as unimportant flights of fantasy, the overactive imaginations of children, are being recognized as essential qualities of the whole human. Without these we cannot seek or find joy, nor can we create or access the genius within us.

Especially in the city environments of today, the tiniest child, even at a year old, is plucked from the natural world. The capacity to attune attentive senses to life-force energy coming from a rich environment of living beings is no longer a part of the active data system. Rather it comes to be attuned to the radioactive color tinted stereotypes projected from the TV. Very young children are exposed to energies of extreme intensity even though they may be passively watching a cartoon. Cartoons are filled with messages of physical dominance, of outwitting the other one. Cartoons give the watching children no modeling of love, of cooperation, of inner teaching that could prepare them to enhance or participate in the world.

Instead, the realities portrayed by television force children into the astral realm of the bogeyman, of the beings who are going to overcome us. Children so commonly have nightmares now. That astral energy coming from the television is expanded and magnified in their dreams to create within them the attunement to an astral world which is not a world where there is the sense of harmonic order.

Because the general public does not understand the actual laws of the astral, people now find themselves unequipped to help their children learn to distinguish or discern in the astral dimension. This sets up the precedent for seeking drugs, because drugs take us into the astral realm which is as real as the physical realm. By the time children are ten or twelve, the content of their emotional themes, of their experience of themselves in the world, is built directly from astral energetics which are detrimental to their capacity to become manifesters in the world. The astral dimension is an environment in which one is constantly buffeted by the winds of chaos, by the appearance and actions of entities outside the self. It delays and confuses the capacity of children to experience a meaningful center of the Self from which they can choose and move in their outside world. This is producing an alarming imbalance in young children which bodes not well for the future of mankind.

Nizhoni teaches the child to understand the qualities of those astral energies, to understand how to be centered in any environment. Adults often fail to recognize that the small child views everything as real. While the adult says, "He's only pretending with guns," the child is learning a lesson which is creating an entirely real imprint within himself that is not a secondary, symbolic translation, but an imprint that profoundly affects his sense of safety, his capacity to experience and to participate in a meaningful world.

To help children growing up today, we must understand the mechanisms of the emotional body, the laws of Karma that draw us one to another, each into our perfect, selected families chosen by ourselves. The small child's auric field is very tentative and erratic. The child has not learned how to control its own energy and is therefore tremendously influenced by the energies of others. A small infant has already learned to probe with the fibers of the solar plexus (of the emotional body) to recognize if the people around him or her are happy or sad or angry or safe. This is an initial practice of recognition in which the child begins to identify the emotions and imprints of the people who are close to him or her. Many children, when they begin to paint and draw, paint rainbows around the human form because they can actually see the dynamic auric fields of others.

If teachers understood, if the adult world were trained to recognize the auric language, we could successfully bring our children into maturity with all of the psychic, spiritual attributes intact, which would be more than useful to all Humanity. The difficulty is that this habit of perceiving each other by pulling other's energies into us, causes us to become imbalanced as we grow into adults. As we pull into ourselves the feelings and the emotions of other people, they become our own. The emotional body becomes energetically, physiologically addicted to those energetic, emotional states of those around us. We begin to seek them; we begin to act them out.

Children are the great mimics who become as their parents. Very often, for their own Karma, they take in the exact imprints of their parents. The daughter of a mother who is afraid of her husband, who is afraid of men, learns before she is three to carry the safe emotional posture demonstrated by her mother. The boy learns from his father to veil his tenderness, and therefore is deprived of the great nurturing heart with which he was born. He himself is forever after shut off from what belongs to him.

Within families there is no protection between auric fields. We take in the energies of our families and become the energies of those models and thereby continue the karmic treadmill, lifetime after lifetime, of experiencing ourselves more as victims than as manifesters, more as within the clutches of Fate than as the designers of Destiny. Nizhoni teaches the small child to use the awareness it has in an appropriate way. When the mother is angry, the child does not absorb that anger, but rather learns from the very beginning to radiate out its energy and to clear the emotional body, so that it can participate with love and a sense of wholeness in the family.

We are discussing the openness and the sensitivity of perception of a very small child, a child who is preverbal, who cannot, through its rudimentary language, express its perceptions or its feelings. Instead of verbal language, the child uses the laws of energetics. It uses the spiritual body, the physical body, and the emotional body to move in the world, in the inner world as well as the outer world. In these early preverbal years there is a tremendous wealth of experience available to the child that could enhance the family and enhance the world.

We begin to recognize the richness of the spiritual body that is so much a part of the pre-verbal child as we watch it attune back and forth between the many dimensions. Infants commonly will begin to stare into the great nothingness and within that stare is the action of perception which does not relate to the three dimensional world, but which supports the child as a soul choosing to move from the unmanifest into our world. Little by little we draw the child away from the dreamtime, away from those other worlds and into our own.

By the time the child is three and a half or four, it begins to express itself in language. The first flickers of its expression, communication from those other aspects of itself, are available to us. Children commonly, by the time they are four, express to a parent that they have lived in some environment before, that they knew the parent when the parent was their child or mate. It is not enough to simply explain these stories as wish fulfillment. We must begin to acknowledge the other real interpersonal dynamics of our relationships on a soul level, on a spiritual level. These perceptions of a child are very significant.

We must become acutely aware that a child is a fully developed soul suffering the bondage of a small, inarticulate body. We ourselves must learn to speak the symbolic language of the child so we can know who the child truly is and what the child has come to teach us.

It is very common, for example, for children to predict the death of people around them. Parents find this very disturbing, especially since very often when a child makes a statement of a negative psychic nature, he or she does it from a trance level. This appears strange and perhaps frightening to the parent. We immediately make a response to any paranormal behavior on the part of children by silencing them, by telling them how terrible they are to think such a thing, or punishing them in some way. This creates in children an awareness that such behavior is not pleasing to us, nor does it satisfy our needs and requirements as to their actions, expression, and personality. It also instills in children a sense of guilt. Of course, some of that anxiety comes from the collective unconscious, the imprints through the ages because of punishment placed on people who had "paranormal" capacities, who were actually often put to death for those capacities. Even though it is entirely unconscious to the parents, there is a collective memory connected to the expediency of showing such "special talents." Most often, parents find paranormal behavior very disturbing and will force their child to give it up or go into secrecy in terms of these knowings.

Our own anxiety and fear of death become triggered when children express a curiosity or recognition of it. We very effectively instill in them our own fear when we respond so negatively to their natural conversations about death. When children first begin to discuss dying and death, they do so without any trace of fear. But they quickly perceive our responses to their inquiries, i.e., that death is a scary subject, that it is not to be taken lightly, that if they say someone is dying or dead in a casual way, we respond with great anxiety and even consternation. They realize our panic about survival and, in reaction, become morbidly fascinated with death.

It would be appropriate for us, when a child says someone is going to die, to learn the ways of helping the child use his or her capacity of knowing to communicate further with the soul of that person. S.he could send the person healing energy or help in some other way. A child who can perceive that someone is going to die has the capacity to help to heal—if the parents would recognize the child on a soul level and allow him or her to participate.

Children often think their psychic capacities are a game. When these games of knowing so-and-so is going to call or so-and-so is going to come today are met, not with appreciation from parents, but with a great energy to silence the child, and orders not to play those games, not to do those things, the child immediately understands that to show those knowings will separate him or her from the love and participation in the family.

One of the easiest means of communication with the multidimensional self is the language of symbols. For example, the use of color to represent certain kinds of feelings or qualities is universally recognized. Children often will comment in terms of colors to express how they perceive people. For example, the parent is reading or doing some mental job and the child comes in and says, "Oh, Mommy you're all yellow". When the child says, "You are all yellow," he's describing the energies moving in the electromagnetic field of the adult. If parents could be aware that the child was speaking the spiritual language, we could enhance this faculty of perceiving each other's auric fields (i.e., feelings, thoughts, etc.) to the point where this human potential could become a great service to the entire world.

If we were to develop this potential, it would lead to the capacity to perceive the thoughts and feelings of other beings. This has unlimited potential in terms of altering the nature of interpersonal and international global relationships. If we know each other's thoughts, if we know the quality of each other's emotions, we cannot then succeed with thoughts of negativity. Learning to perceive auric fields is not an idle pastime of esoteric people, but a very practical application of human potential. Simply by acknowledging that children are proving these skills and, by continuing to train and applaud and enhance the child's capacity, we can bring them to a level of mastery and usher in a new age of enlightenment.

One of the greatest concerns for parents is understanding that their children are not only perceiving their emotional states but are imprinting them, are mimicking the anxiety and discontent of the parents who themselves are searching for a way to protect their children from the negative emotions that are freely flowing in the psychic matrix, the astral matrix in which we are all moving.

One example of that matrix is observing what happens to ourselves and our children when we go into large shopping malls, which are virtual factories of emotional garbage. After a very short time, an adult will become tired or irritable or anxious without an observable reason. The child very often becomes hyperactive or irritable, as well. This is due directly to the spewing of the emotional energy coming from groups of people. We must learn how to protect our children from this by using the tools of consciousness available to us. With these we can explain to them in a language they understand—the language of movement and color—how to become aware of those energies and move through them.

Another factory of anxiety is the hospital, where

so often the sense of hopelessness permeates everything. We must learn how to prepare our children to move within these kinds of environments in a way which is safe to their emotional, mental and spiritual bodies.

There are wonderful games that can be taught children to help them become aware of their auric fields and how to push away negative energy rather than sucking it in from others. There are ways that we can, as loving parents, balance and clean their auric fields so that they do not accumulate the negativity of the environment around them.

Nizhoni has practiced many of these techniques over the years. Esquela Galistena was the precursor of the Nizhoni school. In the Esquela, small children learned to understand these principles and to apply the laws of energy in productive ways. We very often would meditate on the names of strangers and the children, as young as three years old, were asked to tell what sickness was present in these people whose names they were given. It was great to watch how the children would take in the name and at the same time, because their bodies are so kinetic, they would wiggle and squiggle, move around and keep their eyes open and in every way seem not to be paying attention. Yet, when asked to give the correct information, they would invariably give information that was illuminating and appropriate. Though they did not know the names of the parts of the body, they could point and would describe the energies by colors: "It's black in this part," or "It's red over here," breathtakingly describing the nature of disease in people they had never seen.

It is important to allow even very small children to participate in the world, to become aware of the cycles of life, birth and death, the cycles of nature, and the changing of the seasons. For example, in Esquela Galistena, they were always able to call the rain. Here is a simple human potential that could save lives, that asks not the age, the qualifications, the intellectual abilities of a person, but simply asks for the capacity to focus the attention on an octave of participation.

Even small children must be given acknowledgement, honor, recognition that they do count, that they bring great joy to the world, that they have knowing. They are so often right about the perceptions of the world around them that we can seek them out as our teachers. We must acknowledge that they are divine souls inhabiting small bodies, come to interact with us, come to teach us unconditional love, come to awaken us to stop repeating unconsciously the patterns of relationship we have learned from our parents. By knowing them for who they are, we can know ourselves as well, and embark upon the greatest unveilings of education: the education of the soul, the evolution of mankind, and the related purpose of each individual life.

LEARNING TEACHING METHODS: RAISING THE TEACHER'S CONSCIOUSNESS

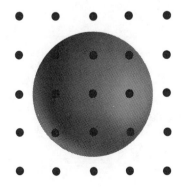

The teachers of Nizhoni are a very cherished group of people who love the subjects they teach and know them from the perspective of the hologram, so that when they are teaching a specific subject, whether it is biology or mathematics or music, they have come to the point of mastery that allows play. They have examined and penetrated their subject to such a degree that they recognize how to transmit it to students in a variety of ways. Indeed, it is the play of all those ways of looking at the subject that allows them to be inspired to transmit knowledge and to inspire the students to embrace the subject material from a place of fun, as well.

When we truly know something, when we have dissected it and thoroughly recognize its anatomy, we can allow our attention to explore creatively the interface between that subject and the consciousness of the student. It is like matching molecules; we discern all the ways we can help the students recognize a connection to the subject so that a student who might be fearful about chemistry, for example, can become so enthralled by some particular aspect of chemistry that s.he will lose the fear of being overwhelmed, or of not being able to absorb the subject matter. Through the teacher's mastery of that subject and capacity to perceive exactly which aspects of it have meaning to the student, resistance is dissolved in the face of self-recognition. The student becomes easily successful.

This is the art of playing. Every teacher at

Nizhoni must be a master of playing so that, as a student finds a point of reference, s.he becomes one with that subject matter. It is in the play that we create genius rather than mediocrity. At Nizhoni we use mind discipline techniques to prepare to learn at the beginning of each class. In that preparation lies the concept that "the learning about to take place is an adventure and is exciting; we will enjoy it, and, therefore, we need not resist." Teachers who love their subject matter are able to do this by simply knowing which of the multitudinous facets of that subject matter will draw the student into the play of curiosity that provides the impetus of learning.

All the great masters used those kinds of techniques we call "sacred trickery" to bring students into direct relationship with the subject matter. In this way, they are not simply memorizing, but are actually touching the living core of any subject. They can then carry this core with them and match up or align it with increments of meaning they find in other classes. They can thereby create multitudinous new combinations of recognitions that have meaning with respect to their lives, that pose possibilities for creating something entirely new.

Not only are the teachers masters within their own disciplines, but their global orientation permits them to view their subject material within a holographic context. They seek out the connections that make learning desirable to the student. By understanding that there is "history in music, mathematics in music", and that we can speak of any subject matter in terms of all the other subjects, we present a multidimensional hologram of knowledge.

In this way, the students at Nizhoni become partners with the teachers. They are taking a basic set, a basic known quantity of information and remixing it, experimenting with it so that they can produce something important, new and relevant to themselves—and perhaps very much relevant to the world around them, as well. The teachers of Nizhoni, then, must also be masters of communication in order to clearly present subject matter the students can easily grasp and build upon. The teacher knows how to enter into the exploration with the student as a clear channel of communication that allows the student to direct inquiries toward the teacher in a way that will facilitate creative feedback between them both.

To do this effectively, the teacher must recognize that, ultimately, "the student and teacher are one." They are one focused entity of consciousness exploring together all possible and probable potentialities of application in terms of any subject. The old totem pole—the vertical structure between the student and the teacher, wherein the teacher disseminates the knowledge and the student receives it—dissolves. Instead, the teacher seeds the knowledge and merges with the student to help take that knowledge further onto a new octave.

We view the basic learning requirements for any subject as merely the building blocks for the actual arena of learning. It is not enough to learn simply the principles of mathematics or the specifics of biology. We must become aware of that knowledge which itself serves as an avenue leading us to a new world of consciousness which we can access.

The teachers at Nizhoni encourage students to assimilate quickly the building blocks and to begin the true adventure of learning which is the application of knowledge to create something new. Therefore, they must not only be clear communicators who are able to communicate the content, the basic material of any subject, but they must also be able to help the student receive this basic communication so clearly that the student can immediately assimilate it and allow the current of energy between the student and teacher to run back the other way as the student responds with new possibilities. The teacher is then able to guide the student to bring forth a creative application of what the teacher has been teaching the student. At times, the student may be ahead of the teacher, as it were. The teacher must applaud the student's efforts to seek new application, new meaning or understanding of any subject matter without the teacher becoming threatened. Like a proud parent, the teacher must encourage the student to be the teacher in any way possible for that student.

The teachers of Nizhoni have, consequently, a very high level of interpersonal communication skills. They are able to relate with students, not from formal patterns of relationship, but from a skill level that allows them each, teacher and student, to be constantly shifting roles. In this way they are continually engaging each other in a challenging yet non-competitive way. Exploration of knowledge is a great game, an adventure of expansion in which the teacher and the students are symbiotic partners.

Because the basis of self-exploration at Nizhoni issues from the strong connection to the Higher Self, interpersonal skills are easily learned and adapted. The illusion of projection and self-identification through the mirror of others is, for the most part, dissolved. Because the teachers are able to play on a very advanced octave with the students, learning at Nizhoni is a very demanding challenge. Excellence is the only possible result.

In some instances, the teachers use subtle spiritual adjuncts as teaching tools. In a history class they may be experimenting "psychically" with historic imprints in order to truly recognize the elements of sociological, political, international realities which frame history. The teachers are in such intimate, profound relationship with the universal truths of their subject matter that they can guide students to explore and discover from the spiritual perspective as well as the intellectual perspective. Often spiritual knowing can enhance and create a more accurate, homogeneous picture of reality than simply the elementary, skeletal perspectives laid down as truth by historians whose perspective might, indeed, be considered "suspect" by their own emotional, karmic participation, their own cultural, personal interaction with any experience.

Our Nizhoni teachers have learned advanced techniques of consciousness which they can apply to surely teach any subject matter in depth. As they teach a class, they are intellectually, consciously, psychically, and spiritually attuned to present the material in a way that most intensely amplifies the subtle interconnectedness between any kind of knowledge and the life force consciousness that is using it.

The major qualification of a Nizhoni teacher is love. Great love and respect and recognition for a young person, with all the magnificent attributes specific to that age group, which the teacher delights in using as tools to dissolve blocks in communication, blocks in accessing the genius, or opening the personal self of any young person. The teacher is highly attuned, lovingly aware of the particulars of young people at this stage of their development and thereby employes these very particulars of adolescence to help the student by using these energetics.

If a teacher sees an adolescent as willful or volatile and therefore undisciplined, and sees those things as negative attributes, s.he cannot interact in a way which produces what we at Nizhoni are interested in manifesting. The teachers at Nizhoni have great love, compassion, joy, acceptance of young people as they are—with all their volatile emotions, all their excess energy, all their tender vulnerability. These are the very aspects of a young person which can be used and enjoyed rather than disallowed by the "adults".

When there is an acknowledgement and recognition of the particular attributes inherent in a young person's evolution from childhood to adulthood, the teacher can use those attributes as part of the play. He or she can orchestrate the volatile, energetic emotion, in a way that allows the young person to use these qualities rather than be used by them. The teacher can create the play. The attributes which in some other environment or school would be considered negative, can be used as an advantage. For example, calling forth the excellence of the young person through the medium of passion to enhance the creativity.

It is crucial to be ever aware that through the veil, the undulating mask of this young being not yet formed in terms of our global society, we are nevertheless dealing with a soul that is more than fully formed, that is purposeful in its choices and greatly wisened through its experiences in many lifetimes! The teacher must always look through the eyes of the young person into the soul of knowing and clear the passageway, open the channel of communication to that great and wise soul. Thus, it can participate fully in the life of that young person, guiding him or her through any intellectual, spiritual, physical, emotional adventure which, on a soul level, that young person has chosen as a tool for growth.

One of the greatest obstacles to communication

between teachers and students is the assignment of roles that are so rigid that neither the student nor the teachers can allow themselves to explore for fear of losing the position that the other projects upon them. The teacher is unable to find a new solution lest the student think him or her unknowing. The student is unable to explore an answer outside of a linear context for fear the teacher think him or her presumptuous to have an answer that s.he cannot explain, even though that answer may be the correct one.

There is a profound commonality between the Nizhoni teacher and the student. The Higher Self is directing each of them and the two Higher Selves combine so that there is a synchronization of thought, a mutual focus of attention that allows for creative genius on both sides. When we are using the Higher Self as the originator of information, of knowing, neither the student nor the teacher need feel ownership and, therefore, can expand the exploration onto many octaves. The teacher need not be threatened if the student asks a question for which s.he has not the answer. There is space within the Nizhoni classroom both for a question that supersedes the material, and for searching, exploring the answer, not from the limitation of one teacher's mind, but from the mutual consciousness expansion that allows the Higher Self to give information that challenges and extends the knowledge of both the teachers and the students.

The game of Nizhoni is awareness of knowledge

and the assimilation of that knowledge to create something that amplifies it. The teacher need not feel the limitation of ownership of information, but can applaud and encourage the student who is deeply accessing the knowledge. An entire classroom can ask their Higher Selves to problem solve, to give them fresh perspectives on any subject matter. This can ignite whole new octaves of awareness wherein the teacher can guide the students into the all-knowing frequency of the Higher Self.

The teacher becomes the guide of illumination whose task is simply to hone the mind process of the student to focus clearly and succinctly enough to bring forth meaning from a holographic repertoire and pinpoint it at its center so it can be utilized in new ways. This is the functioning of genius. All the Nizhoni teachers inherently are of this caliber and are trained to attain this quality of consciousness that models to the student such that each one experiences the self as the inventor, as the creator, as the participant in knowing deeply any subject matter in a way that enlivens and enriches the life of the student.

When a teacher allows the self to be a master, s.he has the capacity to give away the knowing and to enter the play. This prevents the crystallization that happens so much in schools when the subject matter is taught in the same way over and over again until it becomes completely stale for both teacher and student. Because the Nizhoni teacher can keep the subject matter alive by viewing it through all its facets, an unending play of relationship and correlation and amplification keeps the teacher as fresh as the student so that their partnership is a very vital one.

Using Nizhoni techniques for learning helps the students to gather the building blocks, the basics of any subject matter, and to assimilate them quickly and easily and therefore become a worthy partner to the teacher in creating something new. The requirement of a Nizhoni teacher is to take the subject matter into such a holographic arena that it inspires the minds and hearts of all the students, to use the subject matter as a vehicle of communication that creates meaning and purpose within the context that is relevant to each. When teachers use the tool of the Higher Self, this is the very result of their teaching.

KUNDALINI

When we observe the currents of the teenage years, the ebbs and flows and the tremendous alterations of energy, which include personality changes, bodily changes, and emotional changes, we tend to view this time as the most tumultuous in our lives and, indeed, in many ways it is. This epoch of great change appears to be a scene of chaos in which there is no coherent centering, no sense of continuous direction or purpose. If we begin to dissect the various changes, we discover there is a point of reference that encompasses the entirety of the experience. It is the action of passage, the metamorphosis from childhood to adulthood. Because we are multidimensional beings, our transition is not just physical, as in some species, but endowed with mental, emotional, and spiritual attributes as well. If we acknowledge this multiplicity of our nature, we can effect a more graceful passage into adulthood.

There is an energy with which we are born, an energy that accompanies the miracle of birth into body, from the unmanifest, through conception, into form. This energy is divine in nature. Eastern traditions call it Kundalini. Kundalini is an aspect of the all-pervasive universal energy of "shakti," the life force, the God-force energy that has created the entire universe. Kundalini energy resides within every human being and is of two aspects. The one aspect of Kundalini is the common or bodily aspect in which the divine force of life carries out all the functions of the physiological body. It directs the growth and nature of the body itself, functioning perfectly from the moment of our conception to the moment of our death. Its twin aspect is of the subtle level, representing the unmanifest divine energies. It is this aspect of Kundalini which totally transforms consciousness when we seek to bring it from its latent, unmanifest form into activation. If mankind is to take the catapultic leap in our evolution as a species, we must become aware and seek to consciously utilize the gift of Kundalini.

The Kundalini flows through 720 million points of reverberating energy in the body. These are called nadis. They are passageways for flows of energy, whether related to blood or nerves or to the energy of emotional, mental, or spiritual passage. The awakening of Kundalini energy activates a purification or cleansing of these nadis to bring the human body, the human consciousness, onto the plane of enlightenment.

There are seven major energy centers in the body, called chakras. Each of these chakras attends particular attributes and aspects of our physical, mental, emotional, and spiritual existence. The chakras ascend, like evolution itself, from the base chakras involved in reproduction, sexual energy, and self-motivated awareness all the way up through the subtle chakras of divine communication, wisdom, and liberation. They are all interconnected by a great channel flowing through each of the chakras up through the top of the head, thus delineating man's passage from animal evolution to the actualization and the experience of godhood. This is the destination of Humanity. We can become energetically aware of these sacred energies (chakras) only through seeking to align the divine Kundalini.

At puberty, the endocrine system, which is the source of growth and commands the quality of the body itself, becomes uniquely activated. There are two master glands within the endocrine system, the pineal and the pituitary, each of which controls the balance of flows of hormonal energy, balancing the physiological body as well as the more subtle energies facilitating higher consciousness. They command what the Chinese call the "chi," the whole energetic existence of the body, by orchestrating and directing the endocrine glands. The pineal gland is the focal point of spiritual awareness. It is the great antenna which transmits, retrieves, and interprets signals telepathically and allows consciousness to pervade other dimensions. Free of the physical body, it glimpses the hologram which is the source of all wisdom. The pituitary gland directly activates the gonads of the endocrine system, bringing the manifest and the unmanifest energies into contact with each other, thereby closing the loop of our physical and spiritual selves. This is the trigger that begins the journey carrying us through the threshold into adulthood and at the same time reawakening the potential of conscious enlightenment.

When the gonads are activated at puberty, there is a tremendous increase in the level of subtle energies affecting both the emotional and spiritual bodies and awakening new feelings within a young person. As we witness the tremendous miracle of this passage, we tend to view these energies from a perspective of their volatility. In modern times, we have lost our capacity to bestow sacredness to this transformation which is the herald of the future. Puberty is the great mixer of past and future. While birth and death bring us in and out of body, puberty marks our presence and sets the standards of our self-awareness that reverberate through our lifetime. The metamorphosis of the body, in which the sexual energy becomes mature and capable of procreation, is cause for celebration and is essential for us as a species. Even though we may chose to harness that procreative energy, it should not be devalued. The awakening of these energies is, in itself, the gateway to new worlds of possibility which, if perceived, can further the evolution of our species.

When the gonads are activated by the pituitary gland, there is a disturbance in the energetic system as the common Kundalini begins to move and carry out its functions in the development of the body. Kundalini has very often been called the "coiled serpent" because it sits at the base of the spine. It holds the life force energy ready to surge upward and outward through the nadis, transforming our human existence to the very core.

As this energy awakens to focus the sexual energy of childhood and concentrate it within the endocrine system, beginning in the genital area, there is a great build up of pressure or energy seeking release. If it is not held in the lower chakras through sexual activity—which drains it out through the lower level—it will begin to course its way up the endocrine system to reunite itself with the powerful energies emanating from the pineal gland. As it does so, it will purify and open the nadis throughout the body. This is why we see so much flux in the behavior of young people. Literally, all the concentration of energy within the nadis, whether they are nadis related to our mental projections, our emotions, our physical bodies, or our spiritual essence, begin to reverberate with this new energy. Kundalini washes these nadis and empties them so that we may evolve. The body then becomes available for the subtle energies of universal essence. The inner Kundalini can awaken and rise through the central channel merging into the vibrational octaves of the true self. Here is the source of all knowing. We can help ease this passage if we understand what is causing the surge of energy and in what way it is affecting the body.

This great energy rises usually in the mid-teens. It is the cause of the radiant faces we call the "flush of youth" and the deep searching which all too often ends in a blank stare as the profound feelings and visions find no communicable expression in the outside world. A schism develops, accompanied by a silent void so impassable that suicide is a common result. Unrecognized as a natural spiritual phenomenon, the Kundalini recedes to lie dormant at the base of the spine while we emerge into the twenties accompanied by a vague emptiness and undefinable sense of loss. If we could alter the course of this regression by teaching young people to recognize and prepare themselves for these energetic transformations, we would bring about a new era of human awareness.

The clearing of the nadis often creates an abrupt manifestation of what is being cleared. Because it is a pure energetic which is having to utilize the channels available in our multidimensional bodies, we will see its reactiveness, its flaring up, manifesting very differently from one young person to another. For example, if a person has a lot of emotional points of reference, these will be increased in order to cleanse the emotional body. In the chapter on the Light Institute process, we talk about clearing the emotional body. If a young person has a clear emotional body and the Kundalini energy is consciously well directed, a completely new kind of creativity, wholeness, and happiness becomes possible. In truth, these two are inseparable. A young person will not have a clear emotional body unless the Kundalini is being consciously directed because the Kundalini will trigger whatever imbalance is there.

In this way, everything in the teenage years seems to be magnified and set in motion so that all of our bodies begin to bombard each other. Our emotional body influences our mental body which triggers our physical body. This constant interplay creates the roller coaster which presents itself as the etiology of puberty, crashing headlong into adulthood.

It is important to understand how the Kundalini energy directly interfaces with the biochemistry of the body. As it becomes activated, it literally sucks up much of the brain's supply of blood sugar through its utilization of the pineal and pituitary glands. When these function on the subtle psychic and spiritual levels, they usurp the energy of the brain. This energy is in the form of blood sugar. When they make extra demands for sugar in order to have the instant energy they need for such high octave activity, they throw the body into a stress reaction to deliver it so quickly. The signal goes out and the pancreas and the liver must make immediate adjustments to meet the demand. That is why blood sugar imbalances are almost the norm for people working on psychic levels. The biochemical wobble is so intense in the face of sudden spurts of energy gobbled up by the shakti that the body becomes ferocious in its demand for sugar, for instant energy. When a person answers that craving by actually consuming a lot of sugar, a pattern is set up in the body whereby there is an overabundance of sugar followed, in about two hours, by a deficiency. This triggers a desperate shift of pancreatic function to supply the sugar. The result is the well-documented hypoglycemic roller coaster which includes not only swings in physical responses, from hyperactivity to lethargy, but vast swings in emotional awareness which are experienced as irrational irritability, anger, and depression.

It is staggering to contemplate the number of

young people raised on Coca-Cola and sugar who have fallen into this vicious cycle. The biochemical interface with the emotional body is important to understand because much parent/child friction and disharmony could be dispelled if both were aware of this interlocking of the physical body and the requirements of the spiritual and emotional bodies. The sugar-addicted young person coming off the sugar rush will suddenly feel moody, depressed, may have a headache, feel angry, and stop "performing." S.he then begins to generalize everything s.he experiences from this one set of sensations which is primarily biochemical. "My head hurts; it must be math." The young person feels tired and wants to lie on the couch, watch TV, and feels oppressed by the parent who says, "Please come and help me with something." The biochemical swings become the whole of reality while other things, such as school, relationships, and family are interpreted from that imbalance. We are not talking to the being; we are talking to the reactive vehicle.

This is profoundly important to recognize in terms of behavior patterning and the addictive behaviors that are so intrinsic to drug use. If we could correlate it to the biochemical swings that are part of the Kundalini experience, we could begin to learn why. The teen perception of what is true and what is good and who they are in the world will be constantly fluctuating. To help young people utilize the Kundalini phenomenon, we have to take these things into account.

Nizhoni is very careful to educate the staff, the young people, and the parents about these kinds of biochemical, emotional, and spiritual cycles so that they can be supported in finding other ways to balance and thus avoid the wild emotional swings that cause them to feel themselves the victims of mysterious forces. It is the awakening of understanding in their teachers, parents, and the young people themselves that transforms their experience of this powerful time in their lives.

Imagine how conscious awareness of this energy by the student, teacher, and parent can transform the experience of adolescence. We can learn together how to bring the Kundalini up, how to soothe it, how to channel it. Very often, parents, once they are aware, have great compassion. They were young people once and can look back and see how that mysterious energy created so much conflict in their lives. The awakening of this energy in their children, something long submerged in them, is a completion. They often were so entrenched in guilt about their behavior as young people that they never released that guilt and the accompanying judgment of themselves. One of the tragedies of the Kundalini energy is that, if it has no spiritual model, no guidelines for understanding, it settles back down and crystallizes. This is like losing the essential core of who we are because we are unaware of ourselves in a spiritual way.

This is one of the major reasons we have so much confusion about sexuality in the world, why we are trying again and again to stimulate the sexual energy and look for a way to hold a connection with it. Sometimes we think we are looking for love or we think we are expressing our freedom, but these are all confusions. We are working to activate that divine energy and simply never learned to recognize and talk about this energy in spiritual terms. If it finds no expression, it creates a wobble within the young person, a confusion that often results in a feeling of separation because of emotional upsets with the parents and others.

In these cases, the excitability of Kundalini's very nature, which is fiery and electric, causes the young person to short-circuit. This is one of the major reasons young people go so heavily into drugs. The misfiring that goes on in the body because of over-amping the Kundalini charge draws them into anything that will alleviate it, whether it is alcohol, or slow-moving drugs like marijuana, or TV. Before it becomes destructive to the young person or is pushed back down where it has a negative effect, we can find a way to give it expression and utilize it creatively.

Viewing this energy from a holographic perspective is what brings the balance. We have to look at the Kundalini energy from a nutritional perspective, from a physical perspective, from an intellectual perspective, so that its impact on the whole being is understood and supported. As we see the Kundalini dynamics from that hologram, we can rest assured that we will be able to respond to these interwoven connections in a way that allows young people to experience themselves in control and yet untethered and unblocked.

It is a most wonderful thing to create a nucleus, a school that exists independently. We do not have cola machines at Nizhoni; we have only nourishing food. Stabilizing the blood sugar while acknowledging these kinds of pulsations helps to resolve them. Nizhoni emphasizes strengthening the body so that the experience a young person has is one of vibrant health and balanced energy. Given intelligent guidance, young people always choose experiences that support and amplify their sense of well-being and their own capacity to participate on all octaves in life, to be present from a place of spiritual, intellectual, emotional, and physical awareness.

Understanding the Kundalini life force energy totally changes the way we work with young people in the classroom, outside the classroom, and in interpersonal relationships. We simply cannot separate the young people from the effects of this incredible power. It is moving through them and, in a way, it is obsessing them, charging them with that incessant kinetic movement that is so much a part of teenage reality. Until we can take into account this rising serpent energy within the being, we will really never be successful at honing a young person so that we are able to actualize all that kinetic energy and channel it in a direction which creates something concrete. Kundalini is the ultimate source of all talents, inspiration, and creativity.

A very large part of the training of the teachers at Nizhoni relates to these special energies. The whole design of how we plan out a day in the life of the Nizhoni school comes from our deep awareness of this Kundalini energy. The teachers help to structure a daily program which consciously considers which subjects are studied when, the best time for physical activity, the time for meditation to still the body, and the exercises to move the Kundalini up to be utilized and directed.

The intensity of this energy as it awakens is a profound reality for young people. If the teachers are consciously supporting the process, it is a reality that can be utilized to the best advantage for the school itself and for each individual young person.

How we work with the Kundalini on a general level can balance its emergence, however it manifests in the individual. Physical activity is an essential way to help the body move unencumbered and bring about harmony and balance. A young person must move, must be able to take kinetic energy and apply it before it explodes. If this energy is directed in its motion within the body, we can find creative outlets which enhance the capacity of teenagers to be still when they need to be still, to pay attention in the mind or in the heart, for the body is not, then, constantly electrifying them. The Kundalini energy is electric; it has a charge. That electric quality simply, overamps them. They need to challenge the physical body so that the kinetic energy becomes streamlined. It brings joy to them to move their bodies. At Nizhoni, we have developed programs that allow the young people to do that and at the same time be thanked, be appreciated, be honored for the strength they have.

Physical strength in a physical world is still valuable if we simply design creative ways to use it.

There are internal exercises as well, with which we can, by focusing our inner energy, draw the Kundalini up the spine, through the chakric systems, and into the head to open up the capacity to tap into the higher mind. The young person has the potential, then, to function on a genius level because s.he has available this tremendous energy moving up the body into the head. Consciously raising this powerful energy increases our intellectual capacity and, at the same time, our intuitive knowing capacity, merging them so that we can function with true brilliance. Recognizing Kundalini and how it moves and works is very important, very integral in designing an educational system for young people that brings about wholeness rather than a scattering. We will fail at teaching young people math, for example, if their attention simply cannot be focused. We have to relieve them of all the dissipating kinetic energy so that they can focus. If a young person can be taught to focus on math by drawing the energy up into the head, the possibility emerges to function as a magnificent thinker who can easily grasp the inner mechanisms of any subject.

Kundalini is a whole system of reality. It is a whole vocabulary that young people desperately seek to awaken within themselves to help them understand what is happening. If we can bring this understanding to an articulate level, then young people can begin to know how to wield themselves in a way that allows them to manifest, to be successful, whether doing something physical or artistic or intellectual. The more we are aware of ourselves, our multidimensional selves, the more successful we are.

It is this kind of in-depth self-knowledge that makes a person very powerful in any society. Anchored by this knowledge, an individual is not blown hither and thither by the winds of some powerful energy that s.he cannot hope to understand or transcend. Kundalini is such a powerful force. It is integral to our very being. It is not an external force. It is an internal force that does overwhelm us if we do not understand the body's needs in relationship to it and how we can help ourselves in all octaves of our existence by using it.

Most of the typical problems for young people, such as conflict with parents, drugs, premature sexual activity, school, etc., are all symptomatic of not recognizing and being able to manage or guide this energy. We can help young people to learn a vocabulary, learn to articulate and to identify the experiences which accompany the rise of Kundalini so that they can utilize their energy in a way that brings them to an experience of success in life. They project volatile energy outside themselves when they are not helped to name it and are unable to recognize what it is. Teenagers may be very difficult to live with in the family because they are moody, fly off the handle, can't sit still, and cannot focus their attention long enough to complete a task. They are living in a high voltage environment and they react as if they were an amoeba simply living a reality of reaction. We have to teach them how to use this valuable energy in a way that creates action and not just reaction in their lives.

By bringing the parents into the process of their children's maturation in an educated way, Nizhoni offers the possibility of putting an end to the legacy of denying and suppressing the Kundalini. By helping the parents, teachers, and students to understand this mysterious, magnificently powerful ally that we have, we can create new avenues of communication. All beings have had this kind of experience and yet not known what it was. We all have our personal memory of these undefinable currents and sensations expressed by the body but fueled by the soul. We simply have had no available repertoire in terms of spiritual energetics to describe the interplay in the physical plane. For most of us, spirituality has been a concept or a religious discipline, but not an energy that we relate to personally as an experience.

In other parts of the world, where young people are trained to recognize this energy, there are those who have brought it forth and used it in their lives. Most of them are religious—spiritual leaders, gurus, people who have focused their entire lives on this central point, the one little point of the threshold where the spiritual energy enters matter. Nizhoni explores and studies people who are masters, who are able to channel the divine life force energy and exemplify how to use it. We are approaching a new octave of spiritual application. In the past, people who were able to attain this kind of enlightenment, this mastery, have always been secluded, separated from the daily world, and have spent their entire lives training and focusing the Kundalini energy. It has never walked among us. What is exciting about Nizhoni is that, in consciously participating with the awakening of Kundalini, we can now bring forth an entirely new kind of young person, a young person who is so advanced in his or her mastery that s.he can profoundly affect the rest of the world. These young people achieve what has been missing for all of us and can allow it to be a central part of our daily lives. We can now call upon a magnificent force in our lives to help us. Kundalini energy is a very specific force. It can be guided. It can be utilized to enrich our reality, to help us learn and communicate the deepest spiritual levels within us that are always seeking expression. Young people are seeking expression in every aspect of their beings. Kundalini is the most creative energy within them. It is that spark of the divine life force energy. We can learn how to give it expression in a way that benefits us all.

SATISFYING THE YEARNING: WHAT IS BEING SOUGHT THAT DRUGS ARE NOT PROVIDING.

To look at the role of drugs in our lives, we have to enact a bit of history and go back to the beginning of that first swell of drug socialization, or mass usage of drugs, which took place in the Sixties. People at that time were beginning to seek themselves in an expansive way, separating from the world at large and the material, financial realities.

The whole whispering of the New Age began, truly, in the Sixties when people, no longer satisfied with the mainstream, started looking for a new self-identity. They began to cast about for some kind of a new imprint. America is a melting pot, and it is, therefore, often difficult for most of us to feel our roots, to be able to wear one costume and say, "I am this," or "I am that." There was an inner restlessness, a rootlessness that caused people to begin to probe. They began an inner seeking. They were looking for a spiritual healing.

Many found it in Native American roots, in which there was a mystic quality not available in our cement cities. They turned back to the immediacy of nature to find meaning. This led them to the recognition of how to use certain substances, certain of nature's plants to alter their consciousness. They became aware that they could switch into another modality, that they could be a flower child, or a hippie, or an Indian, and lose the traces of their conformity in a new kind of identity that was not limited to the mainstream perspective.

From the very beginning, the recreational drugs, the mind expanding drugs, came about as a part of our natural evolution, a needed alteration of our sociological perspective in life. "Who are we?" "How can we attain meaning and participate in the world?" In the Sixties, people began to explore the expansion of consciousness. This idea, this adventure, was modeled by some of the well-known thinkers, the intellectuals of the country, who gave it their stamp of approval as an appropriate means for exploration of the self.

Many of the psychologists of the day, Maslow for example, began to talk about actualizing the self and becoming whole within. All these new concepts allowed people to begin exploring mind-expanding substances from a pseudo-spiritual perspective. What happened was, the moment someone experienced an expansion of the mind, there was a tremendous jarring of the self-perspective, a soaring, a freeing from the ego-self. A powerful, seductive, and addictive quality accompanied the experience, regardless of whether a specific drug was supposedly physiologically addictive or not. Now, 25 years later, we acknowledge more clearly the bonded links between our physiological and emotional bodies. We can state unequivocally that all such ways fall under the heading of addictive. When the controlling ego lets go and reduces the flow of critical chatter saying, "You are not enough. You are guilty," people experience a godly sense of something bigger than the dramas of their daily lives. Daily life pales considerably in comparison with the reality of being free to soar.

The desire for drugs involves a reawakening of

divine memory, the seeking for something more. Whether we have been rich or poor, rural or urban, there has always been a whispering within us crying, "More. Let me be more." Parents pass this on to children; children are seeded with these thought forms. Drugs have given an experiential reality or reference for that kind of "more." Now we must move beyond this.

One important adverse effect on the body in this search for "more" is seen in the correlation between the parents who experimented with drugs and their children, who are experimenting now. It has been found that if parents use alcohol or drugs as a way of living or coping, children have similar tendencies. There is something in the genetic biochemical balance that allows for a predisposition on these octaves.

We have to remember this history when we look at drugs and young people of the Eighties. After all, they are the next generation, genetically, from those in the Sixties who began the search for the self. Because the drug experience does trigger an expansion into the astral dimension, into realities which can be very seductive and very beautiful and all-encompassing, it provided a way out, a time out from linear reality and the struggle to find ones's place in the world.

Over the last hundred years, in our own transition from a rural to an urban society, we have changed our custom of looking upon young people as adults when their bodies matured. The adult population used to seek out the strong young beings and invite them to participate in the world. This was a part of the frontier mentality, a part of the rural mentality. But, as we have moved into an urban reality, our physicalness has become less of a gift. For the most part, we are no longer protecting, or building, or adventuring. We have become more sedate within our bodies, our physical vehicles. Therefore, we have moved our consciousness, our daily reality, onto other octaves that deal more with our mental body, so that young people who, fifty to one hundred years ago, had a place in society as soon as they were big enough, no longer have that security, no longer are given that welcoming.

Kids today have the best and the worst of it. The delayed gratification our society offers before young people can count, before their lives have meaning, has become so long that it eclipses their dreams. We have bred a generation of young people who have had as models, since the parents have often been unavailable, what is on daily TV. Those models are untouchable. They are always out of reach for the young people watching the hero on television. They feel they could never become that hero, but they begin to experience pleasure by projecting onto those heroes and pretending themselves. The sense of the self and its potential has been blanketed by creating realities that are not available for young people. So where are they to go? How are they to discover themselves?

They seek to find themselves through drugs.

They seek to remove the pain, to remove the limitation, to wiggle themselves out of the discomfort of being too little. They do this through drugs because they have been brought up in modalities that are quite passive. If you compare young people of fifty years ago with young people of today, the probability for being very sedate, even at the height of their physical capacities, is much greater today. Young people spend much more time today being bodily passive. Therefore they build up static electricity which does not find its mark, does not find a channel in which to flow. The agitation is too great for the nervous system. The nervous system is overstimulated and has no way to respond. So, young people simply tune themselves up or down, using various drugs to get out of the discomfort they are feeling in their bodies, in their emotions, and in their minds.

The social structure for young people today is riddled with extreme dichotomies even in their daily experiences. In the home they appear like one kind of person; their peers influence them to look like another; their teachers demand they perform as though they were yet another kind of person. They have so many realities that are not coalescing or interfacing, that being in a drugged state is almost the only way they can feel comfortable. They rarely have the opportunity to be themselves, as their external environment demands so many different roles of them. They are seeking a place of comfort where they are not always being measured or measuring themselves with little chance to succeed at some vague representation of a powerful, successful person in the world.

Even in the late Eighties, becoming eighteen or twenty only gives you the opportunity to be illicit in your reality, to posture the freedom that perhaps is not actually felt inside. You are old enough to drink, you are old enough to vote, but you are not old enough to count because it takes more education to count. As the educational process extends itself, our adulthood, and therefore our expressed purpose in life, is delayed, continually delayed. Finally, when you have your college degree, and then your Masters, and your Ph.D., perhaps as you near the end of that road, your concepts, your thoughts, your creativity can be accorded value by the society around you. Then and only then do you begin to have a stamp of approval. By that time, an important part of you has been buried.

We have become much more subtle, much more complicated with our stamp of approval. We are more demanding in our game of participating in the world, of acknowledging who may contribute and who is not yet ready to give a gift to the world. Being a student is acceptable to society at large and, in fact, a great relief to parents who don't know what to do with all that chaotic youthful energy of the young person who has outgrown this nest and yet has no other.

School then, becomes a holding tank, a storing vessel for something to be revisited after hopefully ripening in an encapsulated environment. For the youth, it sets up an anxiety-provoking reality. Everything is just around the corner: grades, term papers, the next test, the next semester, etc. Nothing that counts is here yet; it is always coming. Now is only a necessary intermediate experience without any authority to stand on its own. Such perceptions totally strip students of a sense of real power. Their very existence is based on an external endorsement. Is it any wonder that lack of commitment is epidemic throughout our entire society? Without commitment, there can be no excellence! Without the full focus in the here and now, little can be manifested, academically or otherwise.

This emotional and intellectual disassociation brings rebellious, reactive energy which results in the classical "drop out." "I don't have to participate." "I won't try because I don't really have the qualifications necessary, anyway." "I can't wait that long." Dropping out is very seductive. It is a defense mechanism against a hostile world. It is a great relief to end the struggle for approval when there is so little support for who we are. Kids become competitive amongst themselves for protection. This emphasis on survival makes meaningful mutual experiences difficult.

Drugs offer the lonely, disconnected teenager a temporary reprieve, a respite from the pressures young people so want to resist. Drugs seem to alleviate social discomfort, allowing the teenager to feel able to enjoy others, free from the distrustful, cynical "adult" coloring that is the trademark of the initiated member of our society. Drugs become a very powerful smoke screen to assist in eluding the sense of lack, the feeling of failure to have an "appropriate" purpose in life.

Yet, underneath this craving and restlessness, there is the true process by which we are evolving closer and closer to the unmanifest in every octave of our reality. The increased desire for spiritual seeking is beginning to dissolve the veil which separates reality from the vast inner space of universal consciousness. Where once only the enlightened sat in caves and participated in cosmic laws, now many are discovering that such awareness can bring the opportunity to manifest as healthy, whole beings.

The world has become much smaller in the last hundred years with the advent of air and space travel. Our consciousness reaches out more. With that, we have touched and been touched by thought forms which are timeless, which are seeded deeply within our genetic codings, within the consciousness of mass groups of people on this planet. We must utilize what science is beginning to unfold, now. Our consciousness can avail itself of the knowing of any other human, and is not limited to only the human, but can actually interact with other species and other life forms.

As the world becomes more accessible to us, we are infused with philosophies of life deeply rooted in other cultures around the world. Reincarnation, for example, proposes a continuation of cycles— birth, death, birth, death, birth—that allows the consciousness a different frame of reference from which to perceive reality. Thought forms and philosophies which include whole lineages of disciplines and life patterns connecting us to the cosmos enable us to pierce the veil of the unmanifest. In piercing the unmanifest, we come face to face with different dimensional realities and divine forces.

The Western world has begun to seek God, or the divine source, or the Great Spirit, or all the many names, East and West, held in relationship to an unlimited consciousness. We have come into contact with techniques which make it possible to move past the paper-thin reality of our daily lives and explore miracles manifested, unexplainable events and phenomena that have excited the spirit, the mind and the emotions of the western world, and inspired us to probe further outside of our own limited lives. By coming into contact with these other timeless concepts, we have begun to enrich our own consciousness and activate the whisper within the western world that seeking God is not, somehow, so foreign or so unacceptable to our nature.

This seeking has triggered an awakening of that which has lain dormant: the unseen part of the hologram of every human coming into existence. It is the divine knowing, the birthright of us all. Everywhere around the world, in all religions, there are prescribed techniques for exploring such a connection. These include techniques such as prayer, rites of denial, austerities, prescribed rituals, etc., which are utilized to release the personal ego. We become so enmeshed in the form and style of our search that the search itself becomes addictive. The ego's need to "arrive" creates the dogmatic routine that becomes the opiate. The very longing which can take us to tremendous heights of self-awareness has focused itself onto a detour that can only take our evolutionary process to a certain limited octave.

Finding our divine connection by using a substance that changes our consciousness awakens within us an association with the memory that was already there. It allows a leaping forth of something that was without form in us, but nevertheless has been there from our birth. At the same time, it creates a dependency and a burden within our consciousness in relationship to our daily lives. Many people began to use drugs as a doorway to their own divine selves, but they paid a great price. The coalescence of the core of our consciousness is weakened by the drug experience. When we take a drug that carries us into the astral dimension, it is accompanied by a loosening of the rein of the ego's control which is always saying, "Be careful over here! Look out for that!" Yes, we lose the nagging ego, but by going into the astral dimension, we also lose our center!

Instead of promoting our evolutionary path, we slow it down. True evolution must be self-induced, propagated from our own inner energy that bubbles up, initializing and sustaining the growth of new consciousness, rather than coming from an external force that creates the illusion of the growth and at the same time exacts from ourselves our own center, our capacity to discern, our capacity to make choices. DRUGS ENHANCE A HABITUAL PERSPECTIVE OF PASSIVE REALITY. We were not born, in fact, to live our lives passively. We came purposefully into body to manifest something that was a part of our own growth. On the one hand, the drugs do open the doorways to expansion of consciousness that allows us to acknowledge and experience something else out there and something else inside us. However, by the same token, we become abusers of that threshold when we are seduced into the notion that enlightenment comes passively or dwells in the astral dimension. It does not.

It is much less painful to live without the ego's judgments, but escaping the ego through a drug experience leads to our not participating actively in our daily lives. This is not spiritual intention. It is, in plain language, a "cop-out," a transgression against the gift of being in a body.

Many of the mind-altering substances create permanent changes in the brain. Marijuana, for example, lays down a sticky tar-like residue on the nerve synapses that cannot be removed. It slows the brain's capacity to flicker into new octaves of consciousness because the synapses, the message carriers, lose their capacity to deliver the data. In choosing this form of altered consciousness, people actually slow down their vibrations.

If we are to move into the unmanifest, we must quicken the human body, the human mind. We must become light beings. We have glimpsed human potential. History has recorded many examples of humans on this planet who have mastered that quality of fast frequency so that they move in light bodies, performing what we consider miracles of walking through walls, of levitating, of bilocating. In the past, we considered this a kind of spiritual magic. In the future, we will view manifesting these skills as a part of human potential that is necessary for our survival. Developing such capacities will enable us to participate on the highest octave available to us. We cannot do this if we damage our electromagnetic field. We are energetic systems.

In order to think on the level of a genius, in order to manifest from true creative genius, we must have integral physical bodies, as well as integral spiritual, emotional, and mental bodies. When we take drugs, we create holes in our auric field. We tear our electromagnetic field, and the aura does not repair itself readily from the damage done by drugs. It simply creates a kind of scar tissue that stops the flow of that energy. We know from Kirlian photography that stoppages in the auric field enhance the probability of disease and energy blockage. Thus, we will not be attuned to the level necessary to perform as masters in this world.

What young people are really looking for is the knowing that is in their own hearts, and the courage to live and share from this knowing. If they can be given the experience that what is in their hearts and in their deepest knowing counts, the need for drugs as an escape isn't there. It is replaced by a sense of personal purpose which is the ultimate thing they are seeking.

Drugs have been used in other cultures as tools on the path to enlightenment. But when drugs are taken out of any such enlightened context, without any sense of purpose or guidance from older, wiser beings on the path, they lose the potential power they have within that context. The result is addiction, states of negativity, and the separation and loneliness that drove the young people to drugs in the first place.

The opportunity of the work at the Light Institute is that connection with the Higher Self offers the true inspiration that allows each one of us to bring back the vibrant, alive, and eternal creativity that a drug experience can never bring in any kind of lasting way.

One of the gifts young people could bring through experiencing the Higher Self without drugs, without the fear and guilt that is created when experimenting with something illegal, is to begin to bring our language to a place where we can truly name these spiritual experiences that we as yet have no way of expressing. Cultures in the East have had names for these experiences for thousands of years, but they are still barely acknowledged in our western world because we don't have a way of speaking about them. Nizhoni may fulfill this hope by giving young people these experiences when their creativity and their physical energy is so alive and passionately searching for a way to make a difference in the world, thus opening the opportunity to our students to make an enormous contribution by finding the words, or the images, or the paintings, or the music that will express these experiences so that our western culture can integrate and be enriched by them.

Another note on what is being sought that drugs are not providing is the experience of the limitless, all-loving, all-knowing self that can move through each one of us in very unique and profound ways. Young people are seeking an experience of that subtle energy not limited to the time line of a particular drug that has its ebb and flow and its negative and damaging effect on the body. There is a way to tap into a much more nourishing, ever-expanding and deepening energy which drugs cannot provide, but that is available through contacting and opening to the Higher Self.

There is a tremendous bonding, healing, and growth that can happen between young people and their parents when these profound life-altering experiences can be freely and joyously shared—especially if their parents are having these same experiences themselves—without drugs, without being afraid of being caught by the law, without the sense of doing something illicit which casts a shadow over any such experience. If the members of a family can share this connection with the Higher Self, the truly profound and remarkable experiences available there can bring great force of positive growth and creative energy into the family system. This can transform much of the negativity that tends to come up during adolescence, and can truly transform the experience of parenting, as well as being an evolving young person, and participating in an evolving family, the family of Humanity!

PARENT/CHILD RELATIONSHIPS: TRANSFORMING REBELLION INTO CREATIVE PARTNERSHIP

In talking about the family, love is often expressed as, "I show my love for you by lending the car. I buy you something," and this is the heart of our relationship. Or, at most, the family sits and watches the same program on TV together. We are losing our communication skills. We are losing our capacity to actively engage in interaction with one another. We have become very stylized in the whole way we communicate, becoming more complicated and separate so that the mind and body are going through channels of equations in order to come up with the basic need, which is to know: "Am I loved? Do I count?" That is the question that remains deeply rooted in the heart of every young person. To answer that question in a way that heals the young person, the parent must participate fully in the relationship.

We understand that, as young persons move into puberty, there is a maturation which demands they find their own selves, find their own identities. They are, at this time, profoundly sensitive to incoming imprints or messages from the outside world which are evaluating them or defining who they seem to be.

This point is very crucial to understanding family dynamics because the young person is, on the one hand, looking with a critical eye upon the life style of the parents and the quality of parenting, which will be either accepted or rejected as a model of adulthood. There is an edginess that happens as the mind and the emotional body begin to evaluate, "Shall I become this or shall I find something else?" If there is communication that implies that the young person is less than perfect, that s.he is not measuring up, it creates an explosive, volcanic interaction or a submerging of spontaneous expression. The dynamic can be such that the parent never knows at which point some slight comment, some small request of the young person to, for instance, carry out the trash or set the table, will tip the scales, resulting in an explosive outburst or cold close-out whereby the young person expresses the underlying currents of separation, fear, self-doubt, and self-consciousness. This great self-consciousness often prevails in the young person throughout the teenage years.

The way in which parent and child communicate becomes very crucial at this time. On the one hand, the parent is attempting to mold the young person into being an adult and attempting to get him or her to behave as a responsible being within the structure of society, while, on the other hand, the parent hopes the child will be able to find secure footing on the path to success—however defined within the family. From the young person's perspective, s.he is, as it were, floating in a pulsating sea, moving up and down and in between a sense of balance and the feeling that success is within grasp, and the overwhelming feelings of utter impotence in the family, and the fear of being without the skills to belong to the world, to find oneself at all.

We have to go deeper than our habitual ways in communicating to recognize these undercurrents

of self-doubt, of self-exploration that are so power-
fully in play and so volcanic in nature. The young
person's hormones are being activated, the Kundalini is rising, the emotional body is wavering with
all of this incredible physical and chemical growth
that is going on within. Parents can learn to be
aware of these undercurrents and their influence
in terms of communication and behavior. Young
people need to experience themselves as "count-
ing," experience themselves as worthy. If the bulk
of communication is externalized to daily "activity," the dryness increases the inner desperation
and the ever-widening gap of despondency occurs.

Very often we have established whole patterns
of communication which become threatening to
the young person without our being aware of it.
Young ears are always listening for voice tones and
inflections that may express or convey negative
imaging, or fail to denote recognition of their
higher qualities. We have to awaken to the law of
energetics. The law of energetics is bound intrinsically to styles of communication. A parent may
be consciously saying one thing, but what is being
expressed energetically may be something else.
This is always perceivable to the young person
whose nervous system is alive with the Kundalini
energy, and as strong as it ever will be in an entire
lifetime, during those years. There is so much opportunity for miscommunication.

We, in our adult world, have learned to become
comfortable with little white lies. We are comfortable in saying things we don't mean, in wearing a

mask of politeness which we attempt to force onto our young people in the name of propriety. These masks are very vividly displayed before the sensitivity of our young people, who are always aware if our words are hollow. They are aware if we are saying one thing and doing another. This creates a confusion for them. The trick to clear communication with the young person is to become conscious within ourselves when we are engaging them, so that our entire attention is focused on them. If we are still running through, in our head, conversations we have had during the day with others, at work, with our lovers, with the adult world, or whatever environment is of importance to us, we will listen or speak only with half of ourselves to our young people. They will realize our attention is incomplete and feel themselves lessened by this. We ourselves tend to give only half our wisdom and half our love.

In order to speak with clarity to young people, we must energetically focus completely on our interchange with them. It can be tremendously enlightening for parents to begin to watch the body movements, the expressions of their teenagers, in order to understand them better. The emotions and the inner turmoil are so readily available on the surface, that if we pay attention, we will ascertain a huge amount of information about what is going on inside them, even though they usually cannot articulate as well as we can. Young people express what they are feeling very clearly through their bodies. With a small amount of attention we can observe these things so that we can palpate the inner feelings and recognize when our young people are in an agitated state. It should be no surprise when, three years later, we find out that our young person is addicted to some chemical or drug, because we have not been observing the signs that are given by their bodies when they are under any influence. We must become sensitive to their physical, chemical, and emotional environments. The attention of our communication with them expresses that we care about them, that we are going to listen to them. Young people want to be heard. Listening to them with all one's attention is a sincere form of validation, and will have a marked effect on their well-being.

More important than the words is the energy with which we approach young people. They are in the process of being birthed again—born. They are birthed at two, at seven, at nine, Birthed again at twelve, and at eighteen yet again in terms of their sense of self in the world. The emotional body of a teenager, even though the outer appearance may be one of, "Don't touch me, don't be silly about me, don't smother me," is saying, "Please remind me that you love me, please support me." They need to be touched.

When young persons go through puberty, parents very often stop touching them because both parent and child are utterly aware of the sexual maturation coming about within the young person's body. Very often a father stops hugging his daughter because he is embarrassed that she is becoming a woman. He is uneasy that she is maturing sexually and feels self-conscious and confused about his role in relation to this young woman who is very active, though innocent, with her sexual energy. A fourteen-year-old girl throws her sexual energy around and wants her father to see it and admire her as a woman. She means nothing more than that with it. But very often, when there is confusion from the perspective of the father, the parent must take more responsibility than the fourteen-year-old in what happens to the relationship. The father often becomes more possessive and more strict and controlling. The communication between father and daughter becomes clouded because, in his attempt to create some safe distance between the two of them, he so often stumbles into the convenience of pretending anger because his daughter has not complied with some household rule. All of this patter and displeasure is really coming from confusion, from fear and anxiety about the daughter becoming a mature, adult being.

The same is true between mother and son. Very often a mother suddenly observes that her son is a young man and may become aware that there is a sexual current radiating from him. Perhaps he is having nocturnal emissions. This again draws the attention of both to this unspeakable, undefined area. They both attempt to create space between them in order to feel more comfortable and safe. They no longer choose each other for company. They no longer touch each other. Again, the negative techniques for separation, at which we are all so masterful, come to the fore. "You cannot have the car because you didn't take out the trash," really means, "I don't know if I think it is all right for him to go out with that girl. What might he do? I no longer have control." The issue becomes a two-way street where it is not only the young person who is seeking selfhood in an undefined arena, but the parent who is trying to find his or her center in the midst of great change.

Even though we might say, "Delay your sexual activity. Behave in proper ways," young people may choose whatever they want today. This frequently creates a painful discrepancy in their lives. They begin to take on more than one hat. They become the student. They are still the child. They become the peer. They become the lover. Secrecy looms up and sculpts separation which very often feels more comfortable to both the parent and the child than continuing the intimacy they experienced in younger years.

Another factor that enters the process is that the parents are put through a reprocessing of their own puberty at this time. There is a re-stimulation of their own memories of how they experienced the sexual energy, their own emotional roller coasters, their own imprints of how their parents treated them. And even though consciously they may have said, "I will never treat my child the way I was treated as a teenager," experience shows that this is exactly what is done. When we become insecure as to how to maintain control or how to relate with a teenager, nine times out of ten we will fall back on the patterns which we experienced at the hands of our own parents. We pass them down, creating an ever elongating cycle of separation and alienation between generations, between parent and child. This does not have to be.

Instead of creating a smoke screen of separation, we can use this time as an opportunity to understand who we are outside our various roles. If we understand the energetic of what is happening, we can nip the separation and the alienation in the bud. By acknowledging the partnership between the parent and the child, we can assist them to move through this passage together. The passage from puberty triggers the parent's insecurity and memories just as much as all the unsettling new experiences trigger insecurity in the young person. Too often this condition of insecurity on both sides creates an unbearable situation for all concerned.

More than anything else, what eases the pain of the young person's self-discovery is a support system of parents who understand the process, the initiation, and can allow the young person the space to explore without putting up boundaries based in fear and distrust. The major tool of adolescent rebellion is resistance. The young person is, as in other developmental phases, pushing at the edges of who s.he is, and against the barriers of behavior, what is acceptable—and what is not. By the same token, the parent is resisting the child who has now become a young person and who must be reckoned with, who may be out of control, a person no longer controllable in the way a younger child is.

Another source of confusion is the unconscious competition that ensues as the parent re-accesses the insecurity of youth. Fathers compete with their sons, trying to convince themselves they are still the strongest, physically and intellectually. Because the auric fields intermingle so easily, the parent is drawn down into the feelings of the teenager without recognizing that he is acting out the drama of the child. The tragedy is that this could be a most fulfilling time in the relationship of the two. For, the young person truly desires to emulate the parent if only the parent would knowingly engage, teach, and model, rather than compete, dominate, and fall prey to unacknowledged feelings!

It is interesting to note that, as a daughter experiences her rite of passage from girlhood to womanhood, her mother is often synchronistically experiencing passage into her sexual prime. While men are at the height of their sexual prowess between 18 and 20, women reach their sexual prime between 36 and 40. This is also when women become most concerned about their attractiveness. For many women, it is a bitter pill to watch their daughters blossom as they themselves visibly fade. Few women realize that they are, at this time, on the threshold of whole new levels of awareness, of sensory and perceptual prowess. Instead of competing with their daughters, they should be guided towards these new sensations, this new awareness and opportunity for independence.

If we can alter the places in which there is resistance from the parent, we can help the young person flow through this initiation with a minimum of suffering. I do not mean that a parent should not continue with appropriate restriction: "You must be in at a certain time. You must be responsible to your home and to your family. You must give time for a relationship with your family." It is necessary for the parent to continue whatever household rules seem appropriate, but these rules can be put forth in a way which does not trigger resistance in the young person, so there is not a gray zone, a combat zone, but that there exists a clear space where the limits are real, and it is acknowledged by all that these limits come from love. Then, within the relationship, there can be a richness and a sense of companionship, a sense that everyone is on the same team.

It is a terribly erroneous, inbred thought we have had for eons of time that, in order to become the self, we must get rid of all of the models around us, that we must break free in order to find ourselves. This is a tremendous confusion, and it will never lead to a fully developed, whole being. As long as we can only experience ourselves through separation, we will not be able to merge into harmonious relationships. If we have negativity in relationship to the parent, we will project that negativity onto our lovers, our mates and our own children. The teenage years are the time to move deeply into compassionate relationship, giving the young person freedom to expand and explore and stretch out. It is crucial for us not to become lost in the maze of our own emotions and our stylized roles as parent and child. We can be present as our whole selves, growing and learning together with our children at this powerful time.

There need not be the element of struggle as young people mature. The struggle occurs because the parent has become so crystallized in the role as authoritarian, and the young person, in attempting to define the self or be birthed, bumps up against that mask. This is the time when both parents and teenager need to release and decrystallize the role they have played for one another. The parent need not grasp harder to control the child. Balanced parents can risk letting go of control a little bit so the teenager can explore. A parent can support this exploration by making sure the child has a sense of being affirmed, by conveying in word and deed to the child that s.he is a whole being, bright, creative, intelligent, respected, and loved.

It is the same dilemma the parent has already faced with the "terrible two's." When parents are confused and have issues about control, they attempt to stultify and smother the spirit of the two-year old who is simply experiencing the process which signals a natural separation from the parent. The focus is, "Let me feel out into the world. Let me see how far my power goes. Let me see where the perimeters are, what the periphery is for me." The adult who is balanced, can enjoy those explorations with the child, can quietly, tenderly say,

"No, this is not appropriate, but this is," and support the child in reaching out without fear. This same process goes on during the teenage years. Parents often resist the child growing up because they are afraid of losing something, afraid of losing their identity as the ones in power!

Here we come to the profound power struggle that goes on in a family. Parents often will slide back into, "I won't give you the car," or "I won't give you any money," or "You must do this for me or else. . ." Whenever, energetically, we are flexing our power over another person, that person will not be able to return positive energy to us. We must learn the laws of energy. If we push the child up against the wall, we give the child no space in which to turn to us when we ourselves really want the love of the child and the recognition of our power.

Parents are in as much of a growth process emotionally as their children. As teenagers begin to seek intimacy with their peers, parents frequently respond with resentment which they manifest as less physical attention and more restraint and even punishment. These outer dramas usually reflect parents' inner anxieties concerning their own sexual feelings. Thus, the parent, while not saying it, signals, "Don't put your arms around me. I am uncomfortable with you now that you are taller than I am." We begin to send out subtle messages about how we want the young person to behave which our child very often takes as rebuke or rejection, and experiences as a loss of the support system. This triggers the teenager to respond with anger, defiance, and bravado. A teenager will feel a loss of love and respond by saying, "I don't need you, anyway. The only thing you ever say to me is, 'Take out the trash or do something for me.'" But we are not confined to one role with another person. We leave a whole scope, the whole rest of the hologram, untouched. As we normally use them, the channels available for us to communicate on are very narrow, if we limit them to "I am only the child to you and you are only the parent to me."

It is breathtaking when a young person begins to explore why s.he has chosen a parent who will behave in a certain way, and then explores the depth of the relationship with that parent outside of the present framework where one is only available as the child and the other is only available as the parent. Suddenly there is a discovery—we have many more points of reference for communication and connection than are expressed within that narrow frame. We can use the outside world as reference points of communication. These become very subtle in our daily lives. Sitting and watching the same television program and commenting to each other is one very narrow octave of communication. Recognizing that we both enjoy music, or that we both enjoy sports, are ways that we use activity in the world to express our connection to each other. Beyond these simple ways, communication can be profoundly deepened when young persons are given the opportunity to explore the nature and ongoing history of the relationships chosen with their particular parents.

It is a revolutionary experience to loosen the hierarchial relationship in which the parent sits on top and controls, while the young person is situated below and resists. When the young person goes into a multidimensional incarnational experience, an entirely new perspective develops. There is the discovery, perhaps, that s.he was a brother to the parent, or a teacher, or mate. These discoveries can totally change the dynamics of the relationship. Not only can s.he can grasp how it is in this lifetime that s.he sometimes has a sense of being sibling with the parent, or in a different balance of power; it also allows him or her to amplify the feeling they are equals. When s.he discovers in the self this different point of reference, rather than the usual vertical stance of parent and child, the young person can remove the self from the limitation and the fear of being the one who is by necessity suppressed by the more powerful one, the parent. This discovery profoundly affects the heart, opening it. It opens up new levels of compassion. It allows a tremendous amplification of reference points by which, energetically and emotionally, s.he can contact the parent—contact that other person, soul to soul. S.he begins intrinsically to understand why s.he reacts in certain ways to the parent. There is a profoundly deeper level when we allow the young person to explore the nature and the ongoing history of his or her relationship with and choice of that particular parent, and their souls' growth as they interacted.

This opens the mind of the young person to the symbolism of communication so s.he can begin to see the anatomy of this dance of relationship. Doing work which opens up the mutidimensional connection with the parent can help young people reinterpret the relationship based on a wider spectrum of data. They learn to see the relationship in a more positive light, rather than from the very limited framework of the parent-child totem pole.

Very often when a young person feels victimized by the parents, and explores on a deep soul level how it is that s.he choses those parents, there will be a discovery that s.he has, in fact, victimized these parents in other scenarios, in other mutidimensional experiences. Suddenly, there is the recognition that the tables are turned, that the one now the child once had the power to be the one suppressing the one now called "parent." Thus, the child is able to awaken new forms of compassion within. There is a cognition that, within the framework of this timeless relationship, s.he is not the victim after all, but that s.he is simply playing out a repertoire s.he has chosen, balancing an energetic of this ongoing relationship. Suddenly there is freedom from the experience of being a victim. The child is then able to release the parents through the process of forgiveness, as s.he acknowledges them, as s.he sees how s.he has treated the parents (who were then the children, perhaps) in other lifetimes.

When we strengthen our own sense of who we

are in a relationship, we create more space for the other person. We can, through this multidimensional work, see how that pattern began and change it so that we are not unconsciously coaxing the parent to play some role which allows us to express anger, allows us to be justified by feeling victimized. Through this emotional clearing there is a dropping away of the old patternings. What is spectacular and miraculous is that, if the young person deepens the recognition of all scenarios relevant to the parental relationship, the entire pattern can be released. What then happens in the daily life after the sessions is that, the parents also are released and stop behaving within the old patterning. They simply stop doing it because, unconsciously, they recognize that the young person isn't available for that particular emotional patterning. This is what is transformative, and profoundly exciting to witness.

Over and over again in this work there is a complete change in the relationship between parent and child. The young person is no longer dictating a negative reality. It is incredible for persons of 14 or 15 or 16 to get the inkling that they are actually creating their own reality. When they learn this, the change is instantaneous and remarkable, as contrasted with what happens with adults. When we talk about creating reality to an adult, the emotional body we call the "rational mind" enters in and interferes, because adults are so heavily invested in being a certain way that they are usually unable to take responsibility and to acknowledge this kind of power.

A young person who is not so weighted down, burdened, invested in being a certain way, is freer and lighter. It is easier for young people to see and experience recognition of the fact that they are creating their own reality, that they do not have to maintain a negative relationship with their parents and that they can actually release them. When we imprint within our consciousness that we are letting someone go, that we no longer need to hold them in the bondage of the role they are playing for us, there is nothing left, no struggle, no resistance. There is nothing left to keep us from moving upward, from soaring, from becoming free of the bondage of those relationship patternings. The teenager begins to be able to embrace the parents physically, to say, "I love you," when the parents have long since ceased to be able to to the same because they are still holding all of the fear and discomfort puberty has raised for them.

There is a dynamic and wonderful mirroring between parents and their children. The parents are saying to the young person, "You must be all that I wanted to be. You must be acceptable," and the parents are very invested in pushing the child out into the world as a successful being where they themselves feel perhaps that they failed. The child looks at the parents and sees all the ways and places the parents have failed. A very fascinating mirroring goes on within this scenario wherein neither one can withstand that spotlight. The young person cannot stand the spotlight which commands, "You must be the one who is perfect and successful," in order to please the parent. The parent cannot withstand the spotlight of the young person's scrutiny which says, "But look, you lack integrity," or "You are not honest; you live with a facade."

We can explore on a deep level who we are to each other without the masks, without the socialization process, without any of the externals, but simply, "Who is this energy to me and how has it honed me? How has it taught me? How has it affected my growth?" Then we are able to see the gift that every person in our lives gives to us. Because our parents are our own blood, they are our own essence energy, they are the most important to us, even though we often grow up and become very different and alienated from them and live in different places around the world and think of them very little. Unconsciously, within the molecular structure of our physical body, within the whispering of the encapsulations of the emotional imprints, we cannot see past our parents. This the core of the substance behind the famous statement, "Ask a man how he feels about his mother and he will tell you how he treats his wife." There is no time elapsed there. There is simply an imprint we continue to perpetuate. We project it outward from our inner self. Until we have released and healed our relationships with our parents, we have little chance of communicating and relating on a high octave with the outside world, an octave that encompasses ourselves as whole beings.

Nizhoni, and the whole of the Light Institute, provide the arena of consciousness that allows both the parents and the young people, independently of each other and together, to look smilingly upon the truth of the choice of their relationships. In today's world, we have many divorced families. We must talk about the result of divorce or step-parents or foster parents because this provides, again, a great smoke screen to the emotional body, a great crutch that we can utilize to say, "You are not of my choosing. My parent chose you. Therefore, I am simply the victim who must surrender or resist you with all my might." When we look at that relationship on a soul level, we discover that though this may be a step-parent, this is not a stranger to us.

During the work at the Light Institute, the student discovers that the parent married such a person in a synergy of balance to bring that person into the inner circle in order to continue some previous relationship. They are perfectly chosen souls who have agreed to enter our arena, our reality, to help us grow. Students learn how we generate a separating process by which the emotional body says, "I cannot be happy because you are in the way. I can't have my beloved father because he has married you, and now I am estranged from both of you." They discover that this is an emotional smoke screen. Perhaps we would be afraid to "have the father" anyway, because there may be some aspect of that relationship which is unseen and uncomfortable. It is a profound gift to explore these kinds of threesome or triad relationships whereby one is choosing another and we must, therefore, enter into the dance with that person. No step-parent has been brought into our life except to teach us, and this step-parent was not brought by our parent, but by ourselves! We are responsible for this relationship, as we have chosen it. We have participated, and it is a profoundly releasing, uplifting experience to understand that we are not victims, that we cannot be kept from relationship with another person.

By the same token, when in a divorce a young person lives with the mother and no longer sees the father, that separation is always purposeful. It is not a punishment brought to us by the external world. When a parent is separated from us, whether by divorce or death, because we are multidimensional beings, the death or separation does not disconnect us spiritually or emotionally from that person. We can become conscious that the relationship continues. In fact, it continues lifetime after lifetime. For example, when a young person has not seen his or her father since s.he was very young and feels abandoned, angry or resentful because of that seemingly forced separation over which s.he feels no control, learning the true purpose for this experience can enhance the experience of being released from the physical presence of that parent. When a parent is removed from us, it is always because on a spiritual level we have accrued enough power, enough wisdom, to create that parental role ourselves. We become the father or the mother, and that energy is assimilated by us. All that the father taught us about fathering energy is taken into our very being; it becomes part of the repertoire we can extend out to the world around us.

We begin to view these experiences, not from a perspective of victimization, but from the viewpoint that it has brought a gift to us which has allowed us to take on a new challenge, to take on a new quality within our universe of relationships. Thus, we can be uplifted. We can be healed of the emotional body's repetitive process of resentment and anger that we have perpetrated on everyone else around us.

The moment we give name to the Higher Self, and explain this powerful aspect of our divine being as it lives within us, young people are able to recognize that their Higher Self has always been with them. They come easily and directly back into conscious connection with the Higher Self because they are still within the energetic zones that avail them of this intuitive energy. They have been using their intuitive knowing, interconnectedness since they were children. It is easy for them to remember the feeling, to remember the presence of higher intelligence. Almost all children have some conscious frame of reference which is multidimensional in nature, either having magical, invisible friends, or angelic presences. These are a natural part of the child's experience of the world. Youngsters limit and shut these presences out as they grow older and become conscious that adults do not share these awarenesses.

The Higher Self is a natural and comfortable experience for young persons which immediately reconnects them to the channels of knowing. The adult usually challenges, denies and doubts the presence of or connection to the Higher Self. Once the young person has been guided to begin to practice that interconnection, he/she becomes very adept at releasing the self-consciousness of the ego-self. To experience directly, whether it is through messages, heard as perspective of the Higher Self, or in energetically experiencing the Higher Self, our students come into the laws of synchronicity wherein, upon pondering a question found in a book, or hearing someone talk about something, they will suddenly have a realization which gives them the answer to a question they have been pondering. Because they are not so contracted in their energetic essence, they are more available to assimilate these higher laws of synchronicity, of holographic intelligence, than adults who have lost their capacity to pay attention to the nuances of energetic realms. It is crucial for young people to experience themselves as whole, to access that great wisdom which issues forth from the Higher Self, so that they can sustain the integrity of their own choices and discern what is right for them as individuals. This is truly the only escape from the pattern of desperately seeking validation from their peers or others in order to move in the world.

The major tool for healing is to wean young persons from polarizing situations in which they can only identify themselves in relation to another being. Essential to the work at the Nizhoni School is our communication and connection with the Higher Self. The students come into actual experiential relationship with their own divine, masterful selves, so they do not have to constantly play out ordinary charades of exploration about who they are and what they can manifest in a framework which elswhere always includes participation or mirroring of another person. Our students learn to be alone, to hear the voice of their own knowing, to live that knowing, and to activate their capacity to present that knowing to the outside world without fear, confusion, or polarity between themselves and other people. The power of a full relationship with one's own higher self releases one from the emotional body's struggle to define oneself in terms of other people or the outside world. Our students become powerful manifesters. They become strong personages who know their own heart and manifest their own truth, create it, speak it, and bring it forth in a way that gifts the world.

Nizhoni's focus on the young person's relationship with the Higher Self alleviates a great deal of drama in terms of their roles within their families, relativity to peers, status in the outside or future world. It supports and strengthens who one is right now—a whole, masterful being capable of making choices, being responsible, and participating in this world. The goals is to be, not passive, not a victim, but to count profoundly in this world. Young people emerge from Nizhoni having experienced and practiced participation. Whether studying physics or Russian or healing or traveling around the world, we are practicing that understanding of the self which manifests beyond roles. It is not, "I am a musician. I am an American. I am a student," but, rather, as a famous Brazilian quote says, "I am that I am, and I find it good." We have deep, spiritual experiences and translate them into daily life. By recognizing that, inherent in the student is the teacher, and inherent in the human is the God, the student becomes simultaneously Knower and Creator.

We can begin to see how this kind of development in a young person is a gift, not a loss, to the parent. The unfoldment has the potential to free us all. We cannot be whole as long as we are struggling in relationship, whether it is with our children, our partners, our teacher, or anyone outside ourselves. We, too, must be able to access our own wholeness so that the young person can evolve and be able to communicate with us on a level which honors the souls of both. It is an experience very few of us ever achieve, especially as parents. To feel true honoring—not cultural role edicts, but the respect and the love radiating from our children toward us—is one of the most enriching, rapturous experiences available. It is a wonderful mirror to look into the eyes of our child and know that the child is looking at us with the love that comes from a recognition that we are two souls moving together on a common path of life.

In contrast, if the parent is identifying or projecting through the young person, then the emotional body of the parent will want the young person to be a mirror that enhances the self. Such a parent will actually sabotage the young person. Usually this is unconscious. The parent becomes adamant about who the young person can become, not because that is what the young person desires, or because that is where the talents are, but because only within certain confines, certain particular roles, does the parent feel his or her own image in the world is safe; and this still maintains a position of strength from which to come toward the child. The inner child becomes insecure and this is painful. It is especially painful as a parent grows older and becomes more acutely aware of the level of success he has attained on the outside world's totem pole of success. Such a parent will belittle or discourage the young person from anything that would threaten his or her own crystallized identity.

When young people understand these dynamics of self-image, they are able to support the parent because they are untouched by it. They know who they are. They can choose what they need to choose, and, in doing so, can gift their parents with love. We cannot always change the chaos around us. If we have a parent who has very adamant thoughts about what is good and what is appropriate, we cannot change those imprints, but we can understand them from the level of the heart. We are no longer bound by them and, being free of them, we then have more energy available to give back compassion and love because we are not threatened by their needs. We can live our life free of those limited perceptions of how things should be and at the same time support our parents by acknowledging the validity of their values and perceptions, wherever they have achieved comfort.

It is a wonderful feeling to be able to accept a parent who is living a life style you do not choose, yet be able to communicate lovingly with that parent. At Nizhoni, we actively focus on the healing and evolving of the relationship between the parents and the young people. We always suggest that parents do this in-depth soul work so that they may experience what their children experience. They, too, have the opportunity to release their own parents so they need not perpetrate those thought forms, those concepts about how life should be or how their children should be. Through this work, they can free themselves first of the karmic patterns projected onto them and, subsequently, onto their children. When they release their own children, they magnify the avenues of communion available between them. Nizhoni provides weekends and special times in which parents can come and participate in the school alongside their young people. We provide internships in which they can go on adventures together and experience mutual sharing, excitement, learning in which neither one has to be above the other, but both can be students, and explorers. We have many possibilities for physical adventures such as wilderness experiences in which the young person and the parent can move together into nature. They can learn to cooperatively work with each other, using the physical strength of the young person who then supports and encourages the physical strength of the parent, at the same time using the wisdom of the parent to guide the young person. Both parent and child achieve a sense of accomplishment, pushing the limits of who they are think they are, what they think they can physically or emotionally do in the world.

Nizhoni is very conscious of providing environments that allow parents and young people to experience each other outside of limiting vertical roles. These kinds of processes reward them for being able to let go of their roles with each other so that the enrichment comes from not having the hat to wear, or the mask, but simply from acknowledging two souls. Ultimately, across this planet, before there will be peace and a new way of living, we must use this primordial relationship of parent and child in such a new way that we model and are able to radiate a whole new kind of being together: a global partnership in which both recognize they have chosen each other and are able to gift each other.

Only by merging with our parents do we become whole. It is possible to move from the dynamic of rebellion and separation, wherein one cannot be whole nor find oneself unless one is rid of the parent, to a new thought form which is, "As I merge with you, then I-You become more whole." "Where there is no resistance, there is no harm." Utilizing all the gifts our parents have given, we can merge with our parents on a soul level. When we merge on a soul level, the daily emotional struggle, the volcanic eruptions that go on within families, truly dissolve. They are unnecessary. They are not a given in the development of adult beings. It is merging on the soul level that allows us to expand ourselves in a way in which we do not see each other as a threat. When we are not threatened by something outside ourselves, whether it is a parent or another country, we can truly align with, and understand intrinsically, our own purpose in life. There is nothing, then, to manifesting the purpose of our lives once we learn how to access such universal truths. Nizhoni, by helping young people and their parents to come into contact with each other on soul levels, profound multidimensional levels, opens up unprecedented realities of personal freedom and global wholeness for all of humanity.

Nizhoni creates an environment that exercises these principles and brings them into reality. It does not leave them on the shelf of philosophy, but allows them to be assimilated so they are actually a part of global living.

EXPLORING INDIVIDUAL PURPOSE IN A GLOBAL CONTEXT

Our purpose in the context of Nizhoni really means our Self experience. It is the focal point from which our consciousness moves in any direction in order to participate. Global purpose is part of our energetic beingness. It radiates out and is directed into any particular point of reference, project, or knowing.

Young people at Nizhoni must experience themselves as a focal point of purpose. Conscious intention is the key. Purpose, then, is simply the conscious experiencing, channeling of an energy, whether that has to do with completing a job or giving energy to events on a global scale.

For the student, a sense of place in the world is urgently important. The value of a unifying focus with which to structure the education l experience is apparent enough. We must create environments which shape and conceptualize the dreams of young people into actual opportunities to participate in the world.

When we are talking about purpose in a global context, we are really talking about purpose and participation as the two major energetics our students experience and have to offer. It is their internal world moving into the external environment. If young people can focus their attention and their intentionality on some particular task at hand, whether it is problem-solving on any octave or simply lending their knowing, their energy, their grace, their capacity to shake loose some stuck condition happening in the outside world, then the gift they have to offer fulfills this octave of purpose.

Through their participation, through their recognition that, by being there in the midst of a crisis, in the midst of a new creative idea, or the midst of experiencing their own energy, that participation becomes the purpose of their lives. They access purpose through their experiential recognition of their focused selves in any direction at any moment. There is a very important teaching for finding purpose through what we do and experiencing purpose through who we are while doing it.

At Nizhoni, we teach students to master the laws of energy and to apply them through conscious direction to create purpose in our lives. We, ourselves, are the point of meaning, the singular, unlimited resource of evolution!

We do not study to reach a conclusion or goal. We study to expand the points of reference within the hologram so we may see how it all connects. In this way, we actively utilize all experience as the fabric of evolution. In accordance with cosmic law, nothing is wasted. Our observation of experiential purpose speeds growth because we learn detachment. We identify with the Self as it passes through developmental phases and not with the phases themselves.

It really does not matter whether a young person has a burning desire for drama one year, and the next year becomes enamored with science. This is simply the Higher Self orchestrating the development of the whole person. The drama that was so much a part of the desire last year can play itself out in the new focus, which may be marine biology.

Young people may see any situation in the world, any reality, from the hologram of their being, knowing they can dramatize, they can communicate, they can express their knowing. They can radiate their hearts; they can access profound intelligence, profound brilliance within themselves to contribute to the world.

Whatever serves as the spark at any given moment will be harmonic and amplified by the experiences to which they have dedicated themselves. Thus, they can find themselves moving around the hologram of their learning, of their growth, and incorporate any fascination they have into this great pot that needs to be stirred. This allows them to become magnificent, intelligent beings. Intelligence is directly related to problem-solving. It is the one who can be creative, who can say, "Here is a block. I will find a way through it," that becomes a master of life. The challenge to the problem is to come up with a creative solution that dissolves it through the art of intelligence.

Anything we seek out, anything about which we are curious, that we want to consume, to assimilate in ourselves, is the vehicle to enhancing the growth process, the educational process within each being. Anything and everything can exercise the capacity to amplify facets of ourselves, whether those facets are intellectual in nature, or spiritual, or emotional. We can interface from a broader perspective with any purpose in which we are participating at any moment in our lives so that our very focus, in any direction, is a focus of joy, creativity, challenge, and pleasure. We have an infinite array of tools at hand to reference purpose through our participation.

Thus, our participation is very broadly based. We can arrive at any point of interest with a myriad of possibilities because we have taught the brain to think holographically, to look at any particular thing, whether it is a global problem or a personal one, and to see it holographically. We go through a process of relating as many things as possible to it so that the choices available to us are greatly expanded. We can bring to bear, in any situation, an incredible volume of information and references that can be useful in the particular situation and synthesize something new. A young person views his or her purpose from the perspective of the joy in participation, from that wonderful recognition, saying, "I know about that!"

The entire educational process at Nizhoni functions from a holographic perspective. We need not be concerned whether the student will be whole in the educational process. For instance, s.he may be obsessed with music and wants to focus only on that. If the passion is music, then we will help that student learn music by attuning the psychic capacities, the inner ear, the physical body to sound. We will help discover the history of music, the search for excellence in music, the mathematics in music, the effects of music in different cultures around the world, for example.

On the other hand, a young person may have no inner drive that states, "I want to become an environmentalist, a world leader, a psychologist, a musician. . ." If the young person has no inner sense of any particular channel, we teach that the self is the channel, that s.he is the vehicle of participation on a global level. It is s.he who is the jewel, not what s.he can do, not even what s.he knows, but the quality of life force that s.he carries within and that can be applied in any way.

If it is brilliance that is needed, if it is a precious intellectual discipline, the Nizhoni student learns how to exercise the brain in a way that gives forth the capacity to perceive, categorize, assimilate, and produce something of value and, at the same time, creates joy. It is not what we do, it is not the props we carry along in life which say, "I am a musician," "I am a scientist." It is the capacity to synthesize the inner perspective, inner discipline, inner knowledge, and to project that onto any arena, any landscape that comes up in our lives in order to manifest a specific reality.

It is irrelevant if, during the entire time at Nizhoni, a student does not come upon some pressing desire, some particular channel of endeavor. For the student is the instrument of participation in the world. It is the specific choice of any soul to incarnate that gives the power to recognize that our very existence allows us the right, the authority, to purposefully participate anywhere—in our inner world, in our interpersonal world, in our international world—in a way that makes a difference.

Perceiving holographically provides the window

through which the student can explore individual purpose because there is an integration of experience and knowing that coalesces an energetic field that each one recognizes as his or her own and within which s.he moves with ease. Holographic patterning of perception allows the accumulation and recognition of much more data than does a linear format. The linear simply takes one piece of data and places it with the next. Thus, it is very constricting. However, when we can flash the brilliance of the mind, this magnificent computer we have, in any direction to gather, simultaneously, all the related information, our scope is much more amplified and much more accurate.

When we have trained ourselves to be holographic in a global context, we can come closer to the elements which actually create change. If we are not aware on the global level that, for example, a particular group of people has a thought form or a cultural perspective, if we do not take in the corresponding cultural, mental, physical, and spiritual understanding, then our communication with those people will be stultified, narrowed, and it will not give us the result we desire.

However, when the holographic consciousness focuses itself on problem-solving, we can see the greater scope, the interwoven, interconnecting data, the angles and facets which come into play. Then we can create change to alleviate the problem. We can even use the problem itself as a tool for enlightenment. To create an evolutionary process, a solution, we must be able to see all the parts in play.

When a young person learns how to think holographically, learns how to *be* holographic, first within his or her life and then in any situation in which s.he is participating, whether it is interpersonal or global, s.he has more tools at hand to direct, focus, and use to create change. This is purpose. Purpose is not something outside ourselves. It is not in the future. Purpose is the experience of being. It is the experience of participation in life.

When a person experiences purpose through participation, s.he has a sense of completeness, a sense of wholeness that allows one to be unafraid. If there were anything that would enhance the world, that would help the world to evolve through this critical threshold we are in now, it would be the dissolving of fear—on the body level, on the spiritual level, on the interpersonal and global levels. When we learn to erase fear through participation, through the recognition that WE are the answer, we will cease to be afraid that something outside of us is going to cut us short, overwhelm us, harm us. We dissolve fear through our knowing, through our very life force, as part of our creative motion.

Nizhoni teaches young people to be unafraid of the choices and judgments of others. Our students learn to lovingly focus their attention on being whole beings themselves. Therefore, our students are able to participate on an expanded octave such as a global level because of who they are, not based on external props. They can contribute, recognizing themselves as beings who have purposefully incarnated on this planet, conscious of the connection of their wisdom, aware of the innate purpose with which they were born. They have grown past the need for an external stamp of approval.

We must acknowledge the genius, the brilliance, the answers that a young person may have. The brain of a 14-year old is much more active, much more joyous and unafraid of problem-solving than the consciousness of a 50-year old which has become saturated with fear.

The world needs young people who are unafraid and who are wise enough to see the relationship between taking a step and recognizing that, in making a choice, there will be a subsequent response. Young people must be able to measure and view the relationship between action and reaction. Thus, they will produce, in their personal and global lives, a balance of perfect motion and repose—a gift to the world.

The world is full of exciting challenges for the student: diplomacy, disarmament, environment, communication, hunger, health, and so on. A student can create from any of these a point of reference from which s.he can explore all of the related elements bound to cause and effect through the spiral of energetic motion.

There is also another octave of the hologram: the emotional effect of a situation on the global level. Students might choose to participate by communicating in a way that helps to dissolve emotional blocks. They may learn to explore the emotional effects of death and dying and disease. They may study the emotional tools which relate to all the "family of man." They learn to recognize the universal emotional challenges that bond us all and that trigger us to embrace or repulse each other.

The grass roots movement going on around the world is teaching us to align with each other. People are singing the songs that release the heart. They are learning to speak to each other through books, poetry, videos, world satellites, radio, computer modems and fax machines. People are connecting to other beings through a myriad of programs designed by themselves to reach across the oceans of space and culture to embrace some indefinable feelings which belong to us all. One of the major points of connection which sparks global dialogue is the universal desire to be healthy. At Nizhoni there is intense concentration on healing at both personal and global levels.

Nizhoni has several revolutionary courses on healing. In one of these we use an interspecies format to teach holographic healing that effectively illuminates the self-consciousness and projection we normally place on each other. The students are more easily focused on the animal because they are not seeking approval as they often do with people.

The world-reknowned animal healer, Linda Tellington-Jones, teaches the children how to deqal with behavior problems such as aggression and extreme fear. In this neutral context they can reflect on their own behavioral tendancies. They learn, for example, that aggression is released by working the mouth and the hindquarters of the animals. The "Team Touch", as Linda calls it, is a technique of gentle single circles which activate cellular intelligence. It gives a direct means of nonverbal communication with the animal. By doing these specific touches all over the animal, a new and very different level of understanding develops within the student that corresponds to how they relate to their peers. The students work on rats, cats, dogs, goats, and especially horses. Priscilla Hoback, a colleague of Linda, graciously lends her award winning Arabian horses to Nizhoni. Horses are excellent subjects to work with because of their powerful telepathic capacities towards humans.

After working on animals and each other, the Nizhoni students have begun to apply this interspecies communication as a global networking tool for peace. Recognizing that love for animals is a universally held trait, Linda established a project called "Animal Ambassador," in which children around the world all share their Team Touch experiences with animals and develop ways to connect and participate with each other. Together they are discussing, via video, letters, and visitor exchages how to help whole nations find further common ground in projects which focus on the well-being of animals.

At the Nizhoni School, we are working to create

a refuge for injured animals that will allow students to develop healing skills and experience a sense of selfless communication with others.

By comprehending the purpose and meaning of a situation from spiritual perspectives, we can utilize the vast energies of the spirit. For instance, through world meditation, our students are learning that we can balance the energies of despair and fear. By utilizing advanced technologies of the higher mind and the human spirit, we can ameliorate any situation.

All of these multifacited forms of communication amplify our deepest spiritual commonality as kindred global souls. Whatever the context of our mutual dilemnas, the purpose is conscious experience of our collective spiritual heritage. The challenge is to find new applications of spiritual understanding in the mundane environment of daily life.

At Nizhoni, we focus the students' attention onto the vast arena of the soul, multidimensionally, so they may see problems holographically and, thus, how they may create innovative solutions. They might want to apply the latest understandings of environmental information to ease a situation. At the same time, they know they can use the technology of the mind to enhance the effect of those physical technologies. We know we can influence the germination of seeds, for example, through our thought forms as well as through the energy of our auric fields. We can apply these spiritual technologies, our understanding of polarity energies, electromagnetic flows, the power of brain wave levels. We can apply these energetically to something we see as crystallized and actually become a tranformational catalyst, changing present realities for the better and thus altering the future.

Each student who challenges his or herself to problem-solve any given situation, especially at a global level, will be able to see it in this multidimensional hologram. Students can then channel their own participation in a way that brings great joy to themselves. Energy is youth's greatest resource— they love to use it! Nizhoni students feel purposeful in their interaction with the actual problem-solving. They discover answers. They are explorers who challenge each other to come up with solutions. They become increasingly adept at utilizing their own potentials, their expanded consciousness, their intellectual brilliance, their physical capacities. They participate in profoundly meaningful ways. They engineer whole new realities based on their own sense of participation, their own sense of purpose.

Purpose is not a goal to be attained. Purpose is a life force relationship that experiences itself by interfacing with all of the aspects of consciousness that are in play around any particular point of conscious attention. In terms of life work, or vocation, we help young people recognize that whatever task they perform, whatever skill they have to offer, they can contribute to global enhancement simply by applying their talents to a global focus.

An accountant can work for an organization which upholds environmental concerns. Through meditation, spiritual understanding, and global consciousness, s.he can apply the inner skill to ease concerns. Within a series of cultural exchanges, a lawyer can focus on consumer advocacy. Through honesty and integrity in mass communications, a copywriter can promote world peace. A student may have a particular talent which s.he applies to a global problem, or may simply have a global consciousness that wants to be expressed through the energy of participation. Both make meaningful contributions.

Recognizing that our conscious energy has an effect on the world creates a tremendous shift in self-value. Studies have shown that group meditations intended to reduce crime have statistical significance! More and more we have come to recognize the power of our intentionality, individually and/or in groups. The applications for using energetic attunement are unlimited: calling rain, dissolving pollution and radiation, promoting safety and peace. Our choices tremendously amplify our freedom. The tools are at hand for all individuals to recognize themselves as global beings.

As we train the consciousness of young people, we automatically create world leaders. As part of this process, we find people are evolving who can bridge political communication gaps to change how we experience ourselves personally, nationally, and globally. It is simply the recognition and application of each person's energy, on a global level, that produces the change.

Humans have created societies in which the life purpose is not fulfilled, in which people old and young across the world have a sense of impotence, a sense of vulnerability, a feeling that they cannot participate, that they do not count. They are trudging through their lives, employing themselves in meaningless ways. Nizhoni creates global health by teaching young people to experience their lives in ways that do not allow them to be victims or creatures of habit who are not fulfilled because they remain unaware of their individual purpose. Individual purpose is crucial to the value of life.

Our reality has very much expanded onto a global octave. It is crucial for the educational process to address itself to that reality. We must answer the global challenges. If something happens in a nuclear way, it affects us from even across the world. If there is conflict between two groups, numerous other people are involved as well. We must be participatory in the world. Helping the neighbor and helping the neighboring nation are the same!

Global consciousness simply amplifies the possibilities for young people to participate in their lives, to recognize that everything they do and think echoes, literally, across the world. We must teach our young people to understand intellectually, emotionally, politically, spiritually, physically that they are part of the world. The world is very small these days. We cannot afford to continue the illusion of the "them-and-us" syndrome. What happens to them happens to us. It is our nature, our human nature to "belong."

We want to belong, whether it be to ourselves, to another person, to a community, to a nation, to a planet. This desire to belong can be a great tool to open global consciousness, to recognize ourselves as citizens of the world. Our heart's desire is to be all one family. We desire to communicate across the barriers of culture and language. This is a memory, ever so faint, of our species. This is the wish of our collective potential.

When young people travel and live together, which they do at Nizhoni, they take with them a tremendous capacity to break down the barriers, to seek the commonality, to experience the compassion of togetherness, of alikeness, rather than separation and fear. We must, in the educational process, teach the value of global understanding. We must educate young people to exercise global awareness, ambition and joy. The world is their arena. It is wonderful and exciting and exhilarating to a young person, to understand and experience that s.he can be an accountant, a healer, a leader in the world!

Nizhoni creates a frame of reference for students to practice "humanness." It sends them on internships to other parts of the world with specific purpose to interface, to contribute and participate in whatever ways become natural and comfortable for them. Nizhoni inspires our consciousness to touch and merge on a global level, rather than to support negative thought forms, negative perspectives that create feelings of isolation, separation and fear. Whether it is exchanging information or music, feelings or insights, is irrelevant in terms of the larger picture. It is the core of the energy of each being to extend one's self out into the world that creates a sense of fulfillment in life. It is a tremendous, ecstatic pleasure to participate with others.

Each individual has purpose in a global context. We were born to be global; we are global in the very essence of our being. When we direct the educational process onto the octave that explores global context, it ignites a tremendous sense of purpose and hope and creativity within individuals. The experience of global recognition, global purpose, guided by the Higher Self, is the underlying context and concept of the Nizhoni School for Global Consciousness.

THE LIGHT INSTITUTE'S UNIQUE CONTRIBUTION

The Light Institute provides a structural context into which the student can place the fabulous, requisite variety of experience. By learning to recognize the attributes of the various aspects of our own being, we can participate consciously in our state of balance. Students discover the matrix that creates the patterns the soul has selected to promote growth. Within that matrix are the points of reference that design choice! Thus, students come to realize why they find some things to be true or how they actually shape synchronistic reality in order to create experiences.

There are four bodies that interact to create the horizon of our consciousness: the physical body, the mental body, the emotional body, and the spiritual body. How much we can perceive and know of the world outside us, and on what level we are able to integrate the data, depends on the interaction and interfacing between these four bodies.

The physical body is, for us, the most present of the four bodies. For a teenager, this body is very much in the spotlight. Because of the Kundalini, there is always energetic agitation in the physical body of a teenager and it is crucial to direct this great force into beneficial channels. The perceptual levels are at their peak as the entire nervous system is on alert to the vast array of stimuli rippling out from the activities of the endocrine system. We humans actually have more than 70 senses available to us, and at the pivotal point of puberty, we can, if taught, identify their specific significances and continuously catagorize them for a much higher awareness.

If these perceptual qualities available to the brain through the physical body are guided and disciplined, the young person can come into contact with the world in a very meaningful way, such that a new species will be born. There has to be a balance between the more active aspects of the physical body and its capacity to receive, to sit still and take in subtle energetic data. If it is not allowed both, there will be imbalance on the side of externalization, and this leads us ever further away from the true self.

The next body of which we are most aware is the mental body, the conscious thinking apparatus and intellectual faculty of the person. The mind sychronizes the more subtle bodies, as well as the biochemistry of the physical body, in order to heighten its capacity to perceive or to problem-solve holographically. We can guide the pulsations of the mental body to produce expanded consciousness and stimulate heightened integration of thought. This happens when the left and right hemispheres of the brain begin to pulsate together. When these are sychronized, they activate the "higher" mind. It is this higher mind that allows education to be a free-flowing, mental process. The brain was created to learn. It reaches out and takes in all the data available, whether that data is coming in visually, through the auditory channels, or through some other process of perception. The brain, through its own pulsing mechanisms, its biochemistry, its hunger to be alert, to be stimulated, wants to be exercised. That exercise can be a joy rather than an ordeal.

The wall or barrier which obstructs young people's capacity to learn, rises when they have been imprinted with concepts of limitation and subtly programmed to be fearful and insecure students. To dissolve the memories and limits, we must trigger the brain into the higher mind octaves and access a level of memory filled with our own knowing in which we learn easily and integrate magnificently. This is the bridge to our multi-dimensional selves. Holographic thought is then possible. It allows the perception to take in data from all angles, problem-solve or to be inspired to create new thoughts.

The mental body can interface with the physical body so that, by conscious direction and focus, the mind can affect the quality or capacity of the physical body. There have been wonderful studies at universities around the world demonstrating that, by focusing the mind to direct the physical body, we can see a result. For example, athletes can direct the body to slow the heart beat or to become limber. We can stop the body from producing cancerous cells, while activating the recreation of T-cells. This is very crucial to understanding how we can use our various capacities to enrich the quality of daily life.

The mental body, however, does not have the capacity to direct the emotional body. In fact, the mind is very subtly controlled and orchestrated by the emotional body. The emotional body uses the biochemistry of the physical body to color the thought processes. This happens physiologically through the solar plexus ganglia, which is in the stomach area below the rib cage. This area of the body is the center of the emotional mind. For example, if something triggers anxiety or worry, it will trigger the solar plexus ganglia which stimulates the sympathetic nervous system and alters the blood chemistry of the brain. This anxiety causes constriction that very often results in a person becoming blank, having a feeling of amnesia: "I can't remember what I just studied; I can't remember what I'm supposed to know." It does not happen because of a lack of intellectual capacity, but because the emotional body, with its fears and negative experiences, pollutes the mental body. To learn, to gather data and to problem-solve at the highest intellectual level, we must work with and clear the emotional body.

The emotional body has its own reality which influences the mental and physical bodies. It is a conscious entity which can be accessed as a whole, even though we think of it often only in terms of simple exterior emotions such as fear or anger. If we explore beyond these palpable emotions, we discover very deep and, perhaps, insidious energetics influencing all our "rational, conclusive" thought behavior. We refer to it as our "unconscious" because we have not known how to access it below the level of its surface expressions.

Until we can go deeply into the emotional body as a conscious entity, we will not be able to touch the source of those addictive and all-encompassing emotions. For example, if we lack confidence in our intellectual capacity, or feel anxious about our problem-solving ability, we should not assume that it is an accidental imprint or thought. It has a source. That source is often buried deeply within the unconscious aspect of the emotional body. Perhaps when a child was six, the kindergarten teacher said, "No, no, you are not learning fast enough. This is not good." Because of the profound sensitivity and alertness of a very young child, the strength of that prediction may completely take over and bury itself within the emotional body. The child then begins to funnel its attention on experiences and data that reinforce the forgotten judgment coming from the teacher. S.he no longer perceives the self as one who can solve the problem or have the great adventure in learning. The process of dulling begins because an imprint has been imbedded.

The energy radiating from our bodies through the auric field is made up of astral energy which is the substance of the emotional body. We think, "I can't touch my unconscious." In fact, we touch our unconscious through the perception of astral energy, the energetics of the emotional body. Astral energy has weight; it has matter. It is what locks the emotional body into its imprint wherein, for example, some feeling we had when we were six is still part of our perceptual reality when we are 50. This is because there is an astral energetic that is constantly repeating the experience. Emotional experience creates astral energy which radiates from our entire body in a cocoon-like field. It is saturated with our feelings and thoughts, constantly processing our mental and emotional bodies.

Astral energetics are electromagnetic. They radiate out in waves, interacting with the outside world like a magnet, drawing in feelings and thoughts from others or from the astral dimension that are similiar to its own. This is a very important concept to understand. It is the whole principle of mirroring: why we pick the parents we do; why we pick the mates we do. We are magnetizing people to us whose emotional bodies align with our own. If one of our themes in the emotional body is anxiety, then we will constantly be attracted to and pull towards us other people who also experience and project anxiety. They simply reinforce our comfort in the horizontal plane of anxiety, so that we can create new situations on that plane. They represent new ways to play out anxiety so the emotional body can project onto them and not be threatened. Thus, it knows who it is. Under the law of projection, the ego interfaces with the mind body and sets up reams of data about who is safe for us and who is not, rationalities about why we feel a certain way, why some people or some countries are dangerous and others are not. We think we are viewing from a rational, truthful, clear way when, in fact, we are simply magnetizing and giving energy to this electromagnetic process that is going on and constantly recreating itself with the same old emotionally-biased impressions.

The emotional body is the most covert aspect of our being, and yet the most familiar. We think we live in the mental body, but w actually live in the emotional body. It is fascinating that such an ancient and powerful system as Chinese medicine heals mental imbalances through the mechanism of the emotional body by working with the stomach meridian. There is a profound recognition that the emotional body is the pivotal point from which all the other bodies dictate their capacities!

To clear the negative imprints which control and limit our perceptions of our capacity to learn, we very often have to clear away and alter the "past." The emotional body is the filter through which we clear and remove these kinds of stigmas. It is not in time and space. Therefore, an imprint that caused anxiety in a child may still be living within that child today. A young person, 16 or 18 years old, who is still reliving, "I cannot learn; I'm not good at this subject," is the manifester of a self-fulfilling prophecy.

To clear ourselves, we must move to the source buried within the emotional body where that seed was laid. What is very exciting about this is that we can change the past! We can create the future by reshaping our relationships to anything we perceive, whether those be another being or a concept of who we are in the world. The actual perspective of ourselves is, indeed, not in the mind but within the unconscious nest of the emotional body. We have to lift it from that state of suspended animation in which it has lost itself in a cycle of repetition.

To replace negative perceptions with higher frequencies, we must utilize the spiritual body, which is the absolute essence of creativity. Without creativity, we can never hope to become whole beings. It is creative life force that keeps the pulsation of consciousnes expanding in wider and wider arcs. Without it, we become numb. We become dull. We move into the dying phase of our life. The creative energy issues from the spiritual body which, even though it is not accessible in a physical way, is accessible in an energetic way. We must pass through a threshold of consciousness in order to recognize and experience the non-physical aspects of our reality.

The vehicle that allows the passage through that threshold is the Higher Self. The Higher Self teaches the linear mind to participate by expanding its perceptual faculties so that we can still orient ourselves as functional, manifesting participants in reality. The finite mind stretches into the realms of the higher mind that expresses the spiritual energetic. The Higher Self is the megaphone of the soul. Through its access, the creative and divine part of us becomes conscious. The Higher Self is able to pluck the thread of our multi-dimensional divine nature and pull it back through the veils so that we have a way to recognize that which has meaning for us and brings us into a state of whole-

ness. This is education. Education is simply consciousness that teaches us how to be in a real way
in a real world, while opening us to the vast, unlimited data we need to create the future. Spiritual
education constantly expands our world so that we
can problem-solve, so that we can be here!

When we focus our intentions in the field of
education, we must be able to perceive that we do
have these four bodies, which are inextricably interwoven. Unless we can comprehend their interactions, we will only educate from a limited
model. We simply cannot dream of facilitating
wholeness until we can recognize the interweaving
of all these four bodies. This is the work of the
Light Institute: to help each individual come into
immediate experiential contact with the four
bodies and the divine dance between them. A
teaching process goes on where by each being is
able to palpate the various bodies and therefore
experience the self from a holographic point of
reference. In doing this, consciousness immediately expands. Each person learns how to be
in the world by coming into contact with the source
which is experienced through the Higher Self.

The path we are choosing in our lives can become a path which allows us to be fulfilled, successful, compassionate, and whole within our inner
beings, while expressing who we are to the outer
world on a global level. By developing a working
relationship to the Higher Self, we can expand the
mind to remember everything we have ever read
or heard or know that completes the hologram of

a subject. A person taking a test in math or language can have all the associative processes involved with cognition, understanding and integrating easily and joyfully available. This brings the experience of success. We cannot only remember what we need to remember in order to "pass" in this world, but we can reshape all of the data that has come to us by using ourselves as a holographic instrument, creating something new from it. It allows us to experience that we have a gift, that we can participate, not simply in a passive modality as students, but that we are instrumental to new explorations that bring meaning.

Education expands meaning. The Light Institute process begins with an experiential, profound connection to the Higher Self that becomes a working relationship. Through the guidance of our higher knowing, we begin to explore ourselves. When we ask the Higher Self to take us into our multidimensionality, to take us deeply within ourselves so we might know who we are, we always discover experiences that originate in what our linear mind might call the past. We come to the ledge where all the certain patterning, the themes of behavior and thought, source themselves. The Higher Self also takes us into scenarios that reactivate our knowing. Not only are we then able to be aware of these interdimensional or otherwise unconscious realities within us, but we are able to participate with them in a way that changes what we call the past.

This is "past life" work. It is simply reviewing

scenarios that express experientally who we are now. When we go into a past life, we are able to pluck the seed of that life or the gift we had which is affecting us now. It is not the content of the life itself that is important, although it is certainly very interesting. All of the experiences that come to us firsthand during a past life session expand the consciousness of our perception in this life. They provide a choice for us. When we are able to interact with choice, we become the manifesters; we become whole beings. As long as we are limited in our consciousness and think that we are only what we see, we cannot really participate in our lives. Our lives, then, do not belong to us. Past life experience gives us a profound tool to shed imprints which may affect our capacity to learn in school, to be in relationships with other beings, to be creative. When we look at the themes and have a firsthand experience of them, we can dissolve those imprints which no longer serve us in this lifetime, releasing us from the emotional body's constant repetitive patternings.

The emotional body is actually driving the mind, driving the physical body, and reiterating itself over and over again. If we have an imprint of ourselves as not being intelligent, the mind body and the physical body will simply mirror the imprint coming from the emotional body. Because it has such a fix on the biochemical processes in the brain, it literally dictates what we consider to be our rational thoughts. This ability to go to such levels of recognition to shift, to dissolve, and to decrystallize them transforms who we can be in our lives today. We never experience a scenario in the past life session which is not playing itself out at this very moment, often with the very same people with whom we have played it out before. When we explore in a past life talents that we have mastered and knowledge that we have held, the essense of those talents and that knowledge circulates back to us. We are all multi-dimensional beings whose magnificent, ever-expanding arc of consciousness can access other time/space frequencies, other dimensions, other realities to profoundly change our day-to-day reality.

Let me give an example of how past life techniques work. A young person needed to complete a requirement in chemistry in order to pursue a particular line of study. This young person had been completely unable to comprehend chemistry and even failed a chemistry course. The very smell of a chemistry classroom caused the palms of his hand to perspire and began an anxiety treadmill, a mental chatter saying, "I can't do this. I don't understand," which manifested as failure in exams. His Higher Self showed him this repertoire: in the Middle Ages, he had been experimenting with alchemy, attempting to turn lead into gold. In that life, he had forsaken all relationships and all other meaning to produce this gold. Hearing of his success, the king demanded him to produce gold or be killed. In his obsession and desperation to comply, he was very destructive to matter. He maimed and abused the laws of nature to transform lead into gold, knowing that if he failed he would not survive. He thus set up a pattern of tremendous anxiety. He did succeed but, consequently, was required to produce more and more gold. The resources of his personal power and his will were exhausted in this effort. His most feared curse, to be unable to produce the required gold, was finally realized and he was killed. He was struck on the head and died.

When this young man came to the Light Institute, he relived this anxiety and forcing of the personal will in which he did what he knew was against the laws of nature. In seeing this scenario and letting his body express the source of its anxiety, there was a profound change in the physiological body. By releasing the residue of anxiety held in his head and body, he gained a whole new sense of himself.

The student re-entered the chemistry class and was able to use the power he had accrued in that other lifetime. Not only did he find himself capable of surviving chemistry, but he actually became an excellent student. In fact, he had a systematic data system which referenced what he was doing in chemistry class today with what he already knew. Once he was not afraid on an unconscious level that he would not survive, he was able to come to it from a sense of knowing. He broke through the barrier of guilt to recognize and honor his capacities in chemistry. Now he is able to understand how the sense of anxiety and hopelessness from that life transferred into this one.

The emotional body was able to dissolve its fearful imprint that it did not have enough power to do what was required of it. The spiritual body was able to step in and help him let go and feel the light of consciousness, the divine flow of compassion dissolving the unconscious holding of guilt, anxiety, and judgment. In this way, the spiritual body produces a healing through its capacity to lift the emotional body from judgment into compassion.

Unlocking the emotional, self-interpretive repertoire is a great key to freeing ourselves from limitation of intellectual accomplishment. Teaching ourselves and our beloveds to accomplish these feats is the only level of education that will change the world.

When part of the educational curriculum involves clearing the emotional body and bringing in the Higher Self, young people quite naturally become manifesters at a new level. We are born to participate, to experience our own rich, magnificent inner world and to communicate that world in ever-broadening global arcs. When young people are helped to experience themselves as clear, they are able to attain anything upon which they place their attention. They automatically become leaders because they are using the energy that is available, to manifest. That energy is involved in wielding focus and intention, by which they are able to bring their dreams into form. Whether it is a song in their heads or a solution they see in interpersonal or international relationships, they can trust themselves to problem-solve and participate in a way that changes the world. That is the destiny of every young person: to come into the world on a conscious global level.

Becoming leaders and successful manifesters has to do with our emotional repertoire about who we are. As we teach young people to face all their thought-forms and their impressions of limitation and dissolve them, we are paving the way for them to become leaders and manifesters. They will do this because of the clarity of their inner perceptions and the expansiveness of their higher mind faculty. They will do this without hesitation because of who they are!

LIVING STORIES: EXPERIENCING MULTI-INCARNATIONS AT NIZHONI

The first exploration of students at Nizhoni is the work of the Light Institute. They connect with their Higher Selves so they have the security and experience of divine guidance from within them, not outside them, in order to orchestrate and unravel all the elements in their lives that are meaningful. They clear away imprints and projections sustained within the family which confuse the knowledge of the Self. Let us look at why this is so important.

When we talk about the source of angst in our lives, it is amazing to acknowledge that being birthed is perhaps the initial imprint of separation. Instead of recording the birth experience as something done together with the parents, we view it as a drama we survived alone. That deep feeling of aloneness and isolation is a major theme reinacted over and over again throughout life. It becomes a weapon to justify our perception of others as distant from ourselves. We begin this pattern by projecting separation and lack with regards to our parents: not enough love, time, money, understanding, and so on.

In the future, parents will learn to use consciousness to bridge the gap of communiation with their offspring before, during, and after birth. We can communicate with the pure consciousness of those who come into birth through us. During pregnancy, the Light Institute facilitates parents in clearing the karmic patterns which might be carried over from other incarnations. Experiments with in-utero communication using selected music, as well as the focused thoughts of the mother, are proving astounding with their results in terms of enhancing skill potentials. This creates a bonding of interest that can heal and erase the illusion of separation and echo the deep, soul-level relationships that exist between parent and child. At Nizhoni, we start by viewing the choice of parents and finding out how those parents facilitate growth along karmic lines. When we experience our consciousness as something that precedes our physical bodies, we can also have direct cognition of the selection of parents or soul partners who best fulfill our needs from the perspective of the soul.

It is a profound revelation for young people who perceive their parents as forces which hold them back to discover that those very attributes they struggle against are the ones which most facilitate their growth! The Higher Self takes them into multi-incarnational scenarios, past lives they have shared with the ones they call parents now. This is so dynamic an awakening as to often completely change the interactions within the family. They are able to treat each other in an entirely different way. When a young person is freed from investing so much energy either pleasing or resisting parents, s.he has a totally new perspective on who s.he is and what s.he wants to accomplish.

Very soon after birth, the infant begins drawing in through the solar plexus stomach area and core of the emotional body, the negativity of its parents. All too often it becomes the receiver of the parental expression of frustration and fear in the world.

These early imprints cast upon the unformed piece of clay we call the child, are effective for the rest of our lives.

My Higher Self gave me the technique of releasing the parents, but not getting rid of them, which is what we have learned to do in our culture. We say, "I no longer need your help. I will start my own life, separate from yours." This perspective denies the spiritual principal that we and our parents are of one essence. Ultimately, we cannot get rid of that fact. We must learn how to use its unflinching truth.

When a young person goes within and asks to be shown the lifetimes, the experiences s.he has had with the entities we call parents, it creates a tremendous acceleration in consciousness. S.he discovers that this person, who frequently represents fear, limitation, and conditional love, is an energy s.he has embraced for eons. Perhaps the parent was even in the role of the child in another lifetime.

More importantly, the parent may have been a lover in another lifetime. A great deal of the friction and separation which erupts when a child hits puberty has to do with hidden sexual feelings. Those manipulating, controlling issues that emerge for teenagers come up, very often, because of the fear by both parties of a sexual connection that is too unspeakable to be addressed.

It's a love that is not just "perhaps we have been mates before" in a sexual sense, but it is an inclusive love that relates to our connection on a soul level.

Once a young person understands that, s.he is able to touch the parent, able to radiate love to the parent without fear, without confusion, without creating something betwe n the two, and vise versa. When you can understand each other on a soul level, it is ok if your parents disagree with you about styles of life; these are just expressions of growth. These connections need to be understood experientially, not just intellectually. The tremendous rift between young people and their parents is very often never mended because they don't have the language to say, "I've known you forever."

We do make contracts. We carry out karmic agreements with each other. When one of us is conscious of it, we can complete the course of those contracts, or clear them through the powerful tools of consciousness. When a young person releases the parents s.he does not lose them. S.he actually gains them. The only way we can become whole is to merge with all our elements and allow that completion to carry us onto another octave. Karmic lessons are not about getting rid of our parents, but about merging with them on a soul level so that the essence of all they have given us through their genetic coding—very rarely through their intellectual or cultural perspectives—can shape us in a way conducive to our soul's growth. When we become conscious of these subtle energy forces, we can totally change the dynamics within the family so that a 14-year old can say, "I am not under the thumb of my parents. I am a whole being allowing my parents to hone me. That's why I chose them." This enhances respect for the Self and leaves space for loving our parents.

When we release the parent, a tremndous block of angst and karmic repetition is dissolved. Miracles occur when young people are shaken loose from the seemingly irreconcilable entrapment of the relationship with their parents. Parents who accompany their young people to Nizhoni partake of a parallel parent program that allows them to clear their children at the same time. A magnificent new bonding takes place and gives them a whole new language of communication.

Whomever we come upon in our lives, we want to come upon them from a place of balance, from a place where our energy meets theirs equally. Otherwise, we will simply project upon them. They will remind us of experiences we have had and we will stay spinning in that everlasting soup of angst. With the aid of our Higher Selves, we can create a change in our energetic relationship with any other person in our lives. We can release them from the constricting script we have assigned them in our movie. We are inextricably woven together as souls who have chosen each other. When we are willing to release someone from playing a specific role in our life, s.he will actually perceive that alteration of energy from a corresponding soul level and change the relationship with us, even though s.he does not know why. This is true whether or not they are physically with us.

The scenarios brought forth from the multi-incarnational sessions which address the inner themes and contracts between parent and child are so illuminating that the young people at Nizhoni wished to share them. Here, then, follows a small selection of experiences that have been instrumental in reshaping their familial relationships, as well as their acknowledgement of who they are.

I have printed them just as they were spoken to preserve the energy, even though English may have been their second language. The words represent only the skeleton of the body of recognition experienced during the sessions. The summary each offered shows the capacity to profoundly integrate the meaning of the lifetimes in relation to the present.

LIVING STORIES:
PAST LIVES
AT NIZHONI

Alexandra Kuntzsch age 16

This was truly the most powerful and fulfilling lifetime I have accessed up from my repertoire of experiences. It is entitled "Lifetime where I was a human connected with my Divineness and Wisdom." I was a 50-year old nun close to being a saint. I was sitting on top of a large hill beca se I had received the message from God that He was with me and that I should look for Him.

This message had made me more wise, and I had gone up that hill and sat there all the time. I was quiet and could easily connect with my inner self. I spent days praying and going on journeys inside. I was actually turning myself inside out seeing what was there. I lost all bad emotions and every feeling of separation. No more fear or anxiety. I was away from other people while I constantly received light from God and from the sun.

I was up high and could wash away everything bad. I didn't even notice the birds flying by—nothing could disturb my place and harmony. People down there saw me and wondered if I was a statue. When I was especially peaceful, I could bring in a part of God inside me. I radiated. The people didn't know what that light was, but thought it was good. They were afraid to come up onto the hill, thinking they were not good enough to experience this, my brightness. I prayed for them and for myself and got all the godly experience in me so that I became the second sun in the sky.

I was still woman inside but a ball of fire formed

around me. The people saw I wasn't sitting on the hill any more, they just saw now two suns. I just went my own way and stayed over the top of the hill, even at night. I was so peaceful and out-of-this-world. I got to the point where I was all God and lost my human form. I was now the second sun so that God could be visible to everyone through this sun. I had simply dissolved all humanity and became God. I never died.

Identification: All the people, the whole world. The nun = I = the sun = God Body holding memories: Having to separate from everybody to merge in the light. Get in touch with God. Color needed is light pink. Higher Self message: Be God and still be with the people—still communicate with them. The white dove is the symbol to remind me that I am the divine. This past life is of great value to me because it so truly connects me to my life source and real essence: God!! Just by remembering this lifetime and the energy found in it and released to the surface, I access the truth of my loving power that always dwells within me ever ready to be used in this world at this very time, to heal my very surroundings.

The white dove carries the message for me that there is never separation from God, no matter where I stand or walk—each step means, not a dangerous venture into the unknown, vicious space, but living the God-being, everpresent inside—a crucial recognition now, in my life, at the edge of transformation of our planet's chaos into ever-lasting love!!

Sylvia Kuntzsch: Clearing My Daughter

Higher Self comes in the form of a rainbow.

She was an angel and we were sisters. I was an angel, too. We were not really incarnated, but I see stones and the ruins of a wall. So we must be friendly ghosts sitting on a wall—friendly, because we are giggling with each other. We had a secret! We were spying on someone—a man with glasses, rather bent over and very sad. He comes to the ruins every week and just sits and cries bitterly. We are trying desperately to get through to him to tell him we are alive and that he doesn't have to feel guilty anymore. He is our brother.

When we were 15 and our brother 18 something terrible happened. My sister and I (we were identical twins) were sitting on this wall with our backs to a rugby game. We were not paying much attention to it when all the players came running toward the wall to get the ball. They lunged more or less simultaneously against the wall. Being a ruin and not very stable, it collapsed and crumbled, knocking us off. On the other side is a precipice shooting down the side of the hill. We fell down, hitting our heads against the rocks on the cliffs. Both of us died instantly.

This event ruined our brother's life because he felt responsible for the accident. He lost his voice from the shock and never spoke again. He only read books. Our parents were concerned about him and set about getting him a job at the town library because he was so well-read. He was very conscientious about his job and became well-respected for his knowledge of books and organization of the library. This brought him to the attention of Oxford University, which hired the mute as principle librarian of the huge Oxford library.

Today he has come to ruin again, feeling very despondent. We try to let him know we are there by touching his face and shoulders, blowing in his ear, and playing with his hair. We are giggling because we have a plan that we believe will help him get out of his practical world and notice us. We are going to mess up his library in the night when no one is watching.

We spook the library and mix books out of alphabetical order. The next day, he thought vandals and robbers had been there. Every night for a week we mixed them up differently. When our brother could no longer find the books people asked for, he became tense and started to have health problems: headaches, asthma, and even worse eyesight. When the director of the university came and accused him of laziness and failing to fulfill his job, he suddenly spoke out. Finding his voice for the first time in 20 years, he defended himself, saying that he was sure ghosts had taken over the library.

The director fired the poor man and he came back to his home where the fateful accident had happened. One day, he said to himself, "I know that my sisters are alive and I can now take part in life." So he went out and got a job as an innkeeper in the village. He began to talk and have friends. Everyone loved him and his health returned.

My sister and I shook hands and said, "Now we can fly on to the next place." We went back and straightened up the library and then went on to a higher frequency to wait for our brother.

My Higher Self says there is a time for everything, tiome to set everything in order. If we have love, it is stronger than anything else and will set us free.

The contract with my twin sister was, "We shall always stick together." The gift I gave my sister to release the contract was an egg. The gift my sister gave me was a book which filled the emptiness in my stomach.

Sister: my daughter.

Brother: my husband.

University director: my husband's boss.

Guests: our friends.

I learned that each of us must be separate in order to be free to function. We cannot go forward when we are held by contracts which we have made with each other, even when it would appear to be beneficial to another—in the case of this story, to our brother. When I identified the brother as my husband in this present life, I realized my daughter and I were working together as a team to solve my husband's problems for him.

We were trying to move him after a pattern which we thought he should follow. This is, of course, not our responsibility and was causing insecurity, anger, and frustration in the family. With the realization that this past life presented to me, my daughter is free to go her own way, my husband can develop at his own spiritual rate, and I am released of the responsibility of carrying other people's burdens for them.

Christopher Kuntzsch age 12: Clearing His Father

In Koln, next to the big dome. I am 14 years old in the early 1900s. I have a girl on my arm. She is 10 or 12. We go into an ice-cafe; we eat ice cream. We talk about our parents. She is a friend. The two families know each other. I tell her that my father hit me in the face today because I didn't do my homework. I have a nice mother; she protects me from my father. The girl told me that her mother is pretty mean to her and her father is pretty nice. She can do her homework when she wants to. I must do my homework when my father tells me to. She is pretty free. Her father has more power than her mother who is pretty mean. If the father tells the mother to stop screaming, the mother stops.

The little girl's name is Wendy. I tell her to come home with me; I want her to see my parents. We went home; it is a big house. My father screamed at me, "Why didn't you do your homework? It's very late." We get scared. My mother came to protect me. My father ran into the garden and my mother gave us some ice tea and was very nice to us. We went to play in my room. We played cards and fell asleep. We woke up, hearing my mom screaming for help. I hear my father's voice: "I will kill you." There's a lot of noise, then it's very still. My mother (who is my father now) was lying on the ground and was dead. My father strangled her to death.

My father sat there and died. He couldn't understand why he did that. He took a knife and killed himself.

We ran out for help. The police and the ambulances came in horse carriages. The next day, I went to school and during the class a woman from the orphanage wanted to take me with her. I ran away to the forest and hid there. At night, it was so cold I froze in my sleep. In the morning somebody, a german shepard, found me with a policeman. My soul goes up into the sky. I see a white field. Everybody is white there: dogs, animals, angels.

Father = my sister.

Mother = my father.

I think this past life is important for our family because I can analyze the reason for our family life before Galisteo.

My sister now was my father in the past life. In the past life, my mom and dad didn't get along at all! So, in this lifetime, my father and sister didn't get along very well either, until now. My sister and father didn't get along until they cleared each other in the sessions. Alexandra had been sad in her other life as the father because she killed my present father and then took her own life. She had guilty feelings in this life.

Mattias Kuntzsch: Clearing Alexandra

I am near a cave; it doesn't change. I am at the entrance of this cave. I go into the cave. It gets darker and darker.

There is a beach. I see a village with some houses. It is evening. I am barefoot, standing near a well. There is no water down there. It is like a big flash down there—like straw. Now it looks like a natural hole. I feel young. I am 15. I am disappointed that there is no water in it. I am looking around. I feel satisfied with nobody around me. I start to walk to the spot in the distance.

Now I fly. I am in bright grey clouds, the edges full of sunshine. I am able to fly. I have no body. Now I can see the landscape, hills, grass. I feel as if I am looking for something.

Now I feel as if I am lying on my back in the middle of weeds. The sky is not yellow anymore. I am just free and floating.

There is a bizarre mountain. It is smoking. I am flying into a triangle opening. It is a very bright beige rock. All over it is like steam. I don't see anything. I float over it; it's gone. I don't know if it was on earth or somewhere else. I feel completely free and I am flying from one strange object to another. It's like looking for something without any will or decision—just floating.

There is a big fat jellyfish. There are rich lamps hanging down. I am floating into the light. It doesn't seem to be allowed to enter. I am outside looking into it. I have the warning not to go in. No will nor desire. I am led around floating.

Now I am floating in a pink cloud. It is not yet space, but in a strange stratosphere. It is glowing like wild fire. There are great cloud formations. There is a pyramid form. I float down. There is a fantastic big volcano, fantastic big flames. I am floating on and on over a desert landscape. All of a sudden, I am in a big cloud—no structure. There are some windows. I go to one of the windows which seem to belong to a huge cathedral. I go through the window. It is absurd. I seem to have a light on me. Someone is lying there, but it is gone. What a wonderful light in that entrance. I see very many things changing—in dark red, as if microscopic. Looking like flashlights on human flesh.

It seems that I am now entering something very smoothly. It is wet and dark and then light, as if I am entering some body, through the veins, and passing by many stations. The light changes; it is yellow and behind it there is blue. There are many layers. Now it is going to straighten up, all the lines in one direction. I thought I was entering a body, something made me enter it. It didn't make me happy, either. It just happened. Now it is so difused. No form, nothing. It calms down completely. Maybe I am a growing embryo. There is mild light around me, almost white.

Now it's all white, as if something is opening like a flashlight. There is a mild material around me. I am looking for an opening to get out. From out-

side, there is very bright light breaking through.
It is as if you hold a strong light on the skin and
it appears to be transparent. Now there is something very red, very close to the eyes, like a vessel.
The blue gets through the transparent wall. I
would like to see what's outside—very strange
bizarre.

There are forms unbelievable, like rocks but no
rocks. There are two holes like nose holes. There
is a mouth. I see a baby's face, a moving mouth as
if silently talking.

Mild light again. I cannot see the body very
clearly, but I think that it is. Now I can see from
outside, but I am still inside the wall. Right now,
I see a figure. I see the mother bending over, having pains. A hospital room, the window covered
with shades. I wonder who is the mother. I see her
nightgown and shoulders, but not her face. It feels
very comfortable. I must be in her arms. I see her
breats, beautiful breasts, but no face. It gives me
very much warmth and a sexual feeling. The light
in the room is like the most beautiful sunshine. I
would like to see her face. It feels very warm and
electric.

There are gothic church towers combined with
high trees; they are brownish-reddish. The blue
sky is very strong. I am looking up. I am at the
foot of the towers and trees. I don't know if I am
lying there as a baby. It is in the highest regions
of the mountains. Again, I am lying on my back
looking up. What shall I do here? I don't know. I
am looking for somebody. I do not think I am a

man or a woman or a form. I feel content as what I am. I see fantastic landscapes I have never seen before. Much more fantastic than the Grand Canyon. Majestic forms. Views into the plains, into a world much more colorful than this world. I float over it. There are red rocks. I am floating freely over it. I don't miss anybody. I am completely content with my floating. I do not have a body. I am not looking for somebody. I am feeling at home with the blue sky and the clouds. Right now, I left everything concrete.

Out of the rude construction there appears a collection of people standing with long dark coats and their heads are like bright lights. I do not see their faces as they are bent forward—a group of 20 or 30. The glowing heads are very prominent. Now, it's all gone.

It was the face of Alexandra, my daughter, when she was five or six years old, sweeter than ever. She was my mother in that lifetime, when I was born.

Mother: Alexandra

Comment: Obviously, I experienced the phase of my soul entering a body, being born and shortly there after dying in the crib. I realized my daughter from this present life was my mother in that life. This shows that we are constantly intertwined with each other and meet each other in many lifetimes in various roles. This shows me that we never lose our loved ones and our continually learning together. This also shows me that the soul leaves the body. In my case, in this past life, I was also able to watch my own funeral. The scenes that I viewed in my soul life seemed to me to be in a higher frequency than the earth's astro atmosphere.

Heinke Burger age 16: Past Life in France

I live in the 18th century.

I see a big room with a lot of well-dressed people, candles and flowers. It's a party in a castle. There is also a beautiful white balcony where I am standing as a young girl of 17. It is a warm summer night. I am surrounded by a lot of young men who talk to me in a charming way. They wear black jackets and not colorful clothes like all the other people. My robe is white and beautiful. I myself am very beautiful and my father is a duke in France. My mother is also at the ball. She is a nice woman but very thin and she seems to wear a mask in her face. She plays a role within the society. It is strange that I am still a quite natural person among these people and with this mother. It is perhaps the result of the relationship I have with the clown at court. He often brought me some flowers and he adored me.

Now I am dancing with a young man who is charming and who wants to marry me. He only wants to marry me because I am rich and beautiful, but in my opinion that is all right. The main point is to marry at all.

Now I walk with him into the garden of the castle and he tries to kiss me. But I'm not really sure I want it because I don't love him seriously. I get nervous and he immediately stops it and stays very polite. Then he looks into my eyes and suddenly I don't know anymore what I want.

—Go back to an earlier time in that life—

I am playing in the garden where there is also my mother surrounded by some men and two lovers who give me presents. But I don't like them because they do it to get more attention from my mother and not because they like me. I like my mother. She often plays with me and then she doesn't wear her mask anymore. But my mother gets very angry with me when I am away because her lovers want to play with me. I don't like them, although it is quite natural to have lovers.

—Go on into a later time—

I am 14 or 15 years old and taking dancing lessons with an old dancing teacher and a musician. I love the musician, who plays the piano and violin, but he doen't know it. I don't think of social difficulties within his love. I am too young. The dancing teacher is really old and bothered by siatica from time to time—this was often a reason for the musician and me to smile at each other when the old man didn't recognize it.

One day I go for a walk with a lady from the court and my small sister in the area where the castle lies. It is autumn and we have taken a white goat with a pink band around its neck with us. A coach arrives and the coachman, who belongs to the castle, asks the lady something while my sister and I are looking curiuosly into the coach where a clown is sitting, making jokes and playing the lute. When the coach goes on to the castle, we ask the lady to go back with us because we want to see the new clown. He comes from another castle because they have had tow clowns before. At the castle we meet our father who is friendly and joking a bit with us.

—Go into a later time—

I am already married to the young man I danced with at my first ball. My life is still full of luxury and my husband is very interested in outside political things. We live only for the society. We don't have parties to have fun, but to be present in society and to play our roles within it.

The clown has been watching my life with sadness. He has seen how I have changed from the happy young girl into a mask of society. He still knows how much I like pretty things. I get bouquets of white roses now and this has become habitual with me.

One day the clown comes to me. I have my own room with a beautiful white window. He brings me a small blue flower from an outside field. It is so beautiful and tender that I remember earlier times. I start crying because I see now how I have changed.

I also know how bad the conditions are in France (in the time of the French Revolution), but I can't help them.

I look into my mirror and I hate my face because it looks like the face of my mother, although I do not look like her. But I have put on the same kind of mask as she has. The "grande dam" with lots of make-up and powder and sad unliving eyes.

Once I was hurt by my husband because I broke through the limitation of society.

We are at a ball where we meet a lady who also was at my first ball. She said, "I am happy to see how well you are dressed and styled today." It was her revenge. At the first ball she was jealous of the natural, beautiful girl and now that girl had become like she herself was. No one but me could see the cruelty that lay within those words.

I can't answer anything. I stare at her. Then I run out of the castle until my styled hair feels more free. I jump into our coach and give the order to drive home immediately. There, I went into my small room. But my husband follows me, full of anger because everybody speaks of my behavior. He hurts me and I don't defend myself because no one can help me. It was the first time I recognized that I didn't want to live in this way. But I couldn't get out of that life and I started hating it more and more.

The clown was also hurt by my husband. He makes jokes and throws down a vase by mistake so the it breaks. My husband gets very angry although we have got a lot of vases and stuff, and he hurts him with a whip. I try to stop him from doing it but he is stronger than me and if there had not been servants in the room, he would have hurt me also.

Both of us, my husband and me, get killed in the revolution. The mad people come to our castle, take us, the other aristocrats and valuable things out and burn the castle. They let the servants go.

In a way I thought that being killed and taken out of the hated life was all right. I also didn't know what happened to the clown that I had taken from the court of my parents to my husband's castle because they didn't like him anymore.

The clown was my mother. As she also was in other past lives of mine, she was someone I wasn't very connected to physically. But she was a kind of turning point. Through her, I discovered how I had become a doll of society. Her role was perfectly chosen because no one else could have shown me this in a better way. She knew me also when I was a child and had enough distance from society to see objectively my changing.

My Higher Self said of this past life, "Why did you ask everybody but not yourself."

It is a central theme in this lifetime now. I remember that once I wrote into my diary about my ballet teacher, "Why does she believe everybody but not me."

So, I think that I am working on the same problem in this lifetime as in the one I had in France and with the same people: Clown: my mother.

The lady: my ballet teacher.

Husband: my girl friend.

They are with me to solve it for all of us. I completely solved my relationship with my ballet teacher. When I saw her the first time again after the session, I felt suddenly love for her. It's wonderful!

COMPLETING THE HOLOGRAM

The kind of people we create at Nizhoni will not be molded into some artificially structured framework which does not support or answer the soul's desire. Right from the start, what we hope to unleash is a fully developed being who can access any octave of reality, any path of life with grace. This person could be a happy carpenter, or the president of anything.

Nizhonis are the inventors, the explorers, the manifesters. They are the problem solvers who extend the edges of the world as we know it. This is why they have so much to give. They have contacted purpose in life. They already know how to orchestrate change in a way that enriches, rather than being taught to maintain the status quo. They are encouraged to push the periphery of possibilities so that new choices are available to Humanity at a global level. They leave Nizhoni with clear vision to recognize and manage global complexitities. World finance, politics, and government must shift to reflect the multi-dimensional perspectives inclusive of cause and effect, responsibly synthesizing human potential into viable support systems, global in scope, compassionately human in focus. The future will be designed by an evolutionarily advanced species of conscious beings!

Fluidity of thought is a necessary component of holographic awareness. The element of motion allows us to directly experience the convergence of polarity through which turgid, dogmatic lifestyles are dissolved. Our dogmas come from our personal, emotional, social imprints. We must not focus on our separateness as individuals, as members of families, as citizens of states or countries, or on our lack of power in relation to another person or group.

Nizhoni graduates are able to access profound power and energy that is available once we sit in the place of knowing. They are not programmed to wait to be received, but to utilize what they have to offer. Functioning not only from a genius perspective, but simultaneously accessing our creative spiritual nature, we have the capacity to read the heart of humanity. When we know the heart of Man, we are able to dissolve and decrystalize points of conflict and fear. We understand what is needed. This is global consciousness. We are not Americans or Russians, men or women. We are whole beings who can live together in a way that allows each of us to uphold our own reality without inflicting negativity on any other. A philosophy of a new education, a new kind of human reality must include our spiritual essence, which we begin to practice by coming into contact with such divine energies as the Higher Self.

How might a graduate of Nizhoni make a greater contribution to the world than a graduate of a more conventional school? The crux of the difference is that a person coming from a traditional school is likely to perceive the self in a limited fashion, in a way that says s.he is still concerned about meeting the standards of the status quo, rather than being an individual who is the knower, who recognizes that s.he has the capacity to garner any piece of information or problem solve in a way that enhances and enriches reality. It is the presentation of that person as s.he leaves Nizhoni which says, "I am here to participate in the world. I am not waiting for the world to choose me."

We are not computers. We are manifesting beings of Light. We have the capacity to give gifts, to sit in the place of knowing. There are various standard career roads. Nizhoni graduates are encouraged to both look beyond those roads and to revamp the status quo. This is the gift of the young: to find new ways to live, to reach new heights. If we have traveled to the moon, let us travel to the outer planets. Let us travel through galaxies. Let us bring back information to enrich life on Earth. Nizhoni students are being trained as leaders, the best and the brightest.

Recognition of our interconnectedness is a major factor influencing the future of us all. The higher human virtues, such as integrity and ethics, will become a way of life only as our internal emotional fear for survival is replaced with the joyous reward of cooperative alliance. We can bridge the gaps and bring our understanding into sync with each other.

There is an enormous need in many branches of government and industry for a spiritual base which assumes a strong level of integrity and ethics. This is where we approach global consciousness. In order to function in an enlightened way on a global level, we must release old, stale, negative, destructive thought forms such as "king of the mountain." We have to understand how to work harmoniously in the world. There is a gift the Nizhoni graduate has to offer: each one is a point of reference, a model of ethical living. Nizhoni graduates do not need to override or take away from another being. They are unlimited in themselves and they are able to experience, to manifest, and demonstrate their reality. When we expand our consciousness, we become global beings. Nizhoni, by training this magnificent octave of human potential, will allow each being to become a happy and whole being by fulfilling his or her destiny.

When young people have a central point of reference, a still point within themselves, and a full connection with their Higher Selves, they are able to live in a way that makes them peaceful, happy beings. As they go out into the world, not struggling, not grabbing for something, not with guilt or uncertainty, they will affect multitudes. They will be able to step forth from the place of knowing into any circumstance or situation that presents itself. They will be a light, a model that allows others to find light within themselves as well.

A state of profound inner harmony creates the outer harmony between people around the world. When the inner being is harmonious, that energy radiates from the person. It is precisely the gift this new kind of educational system offers to all its students and all the families, friends, and acquantances of theses students as the wave ripples out. It is a perception of Self that is not constricted by negativity, but is peaceful. Once peace is instilled in us, we no longer find the world a hostile place. We are able to go forth joyfully with a sense of adventure but also with a very profound core that will see us through negativity. We are able to pierce the darkness, the separation, and find the place of meeting.

We at Nizhoni teach our students to find that place of meeting. An individual does not have to be physically out there in the world to create that which is the deepest soul's desire, and bring it forth in a way that interfaces with and gifts the world. The future will confirm that the reason all of us are so inactive on a global level is that we have been instilled with negative tapes, negatively programmed, in terms of our capacity to participate on a global level. We are simply afraid! We must clear and erase the illusion that inertia is a choice.

Nizhoni provides for its students the technology to release what we call personal karma, or the focus on the self, and directs their talents to the vast opportunities of the global arena. Young people coming in were born to participate on a global level.

Part of the curriculum at Nizhoni is to carry out the education of young people in an international, multi-cultural setting. Students go to other countries and into new environments to practice such skills as personal, social, and environmental healing, cross-cultural communication and universal language symboligies based on the inclusion of our commonality as a global family. They have a complete social, political, spiritual groundwork, a stable centering that teaches them how to function in the world. They learn how to go into a community and recognize what is happening in that community. They learn to go into another country and integrate themselves, even how to merge themselves with the natural environment, such as the ocean. Having learned those kinds of skills, they do not view applying for a job or applying at another school as a fearful situation. They have consciously removed fear as a reality. Can you imagine how profound it is to remove fear from ourselves?!

Their awareness of the world will be totally differnt because it will be integrated into a real picture, not some linear task that they must perform. We give the Nizhoni graduates skills that will not only allow them to interact with the world around them, but to gift the world.

This is a very different experience from being impinged upon by an overwhelming exterior world. It is wonderful for young people to go the Soviet Union, for example, and understand it. The young Soviets are dealing with the same energies. They are dealing with their Kundalini, their emotions, their hopes and fears about the future, just as are all young people. When people, young or old, interact on a global level, geography has meaning, the world has meaning. They themselves are expanding to care about the outside world because the inner world is healthy and whole. The future is as limitless as the soul!

HUMANITY

LITERACY

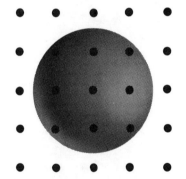

by Alexander Petofi
Director, Nizhoni School

Education is Humanity's primary social tool for preparing our descendants to inherit the future. Given that human culture is changing at an accelerating rate, we should question whether our world system of education is keeping pace with our social transformation. New systems and schools are being discussed and developed, to span the gaps and fill the emerging niches in the rising culture. Which one of these will be our archetype, our mutually admired model for all Humanity? Our hope is that the concerned people of earth will come to know Nizhoni as such through its curriculum.

At the core of our formal teachings is a new subject with relevance to all people: Humanity Literacy.

Humanity Literacy is that body of knowledge which every human should possess to thrive and grow in our complex, interdependent world. It relates to aspects and attributes of Humanity as a whole, and includes the requisite information needed to comfortably be a responsible global citizen and habitually act for the greatest good. Nizhoni: The School for Global Consciousness seeks to develop global citizens fully capable of riding, and guiding, the wave of transformation. More than citizens, we aim to bring forth pathfinders and leaders who can draw upon their inner wisdom, their Higher Selves, to guide us toward an unprecedented Millennium of Cooperation. These new leaders will know how to sense and incorporate the dreams, aspirations, and values of other people while using the great integrative systems, such as business, politics, science, and the media, to bring about socially fulfilling change.

Nizhoni students progress along this path to leadership with an edge, an advantage, over other high school students: they can communicate! While the majority of ordinary students often feel and say, "Nobody understands me," a Nizhoni student, after Humanity Literacy and internships in different countries, will say with confidence, "Everyone understands me." This ability to enter into dialogue with any other person opens the possibility to enter into relationship, and increases the probability that friendship will result. And if each converser understands Humanity Literacy, the energy-dissipating trivia and "ice-breakers," can often be dispensed with, and each person can focus on what she or he feels is important and urgent.

Clearly, there is on Earth an unfulfilled need for a cohesive, co-adapted body of values, around which people can communicate, work cooperatively, and lead or faithfully follow. In order to understand the values of other people, we have to interactively communicate. To communicate vital, complex knowledge that impels action, we must have a common frame of reference, or better still, a frame of reverence.

At Nizhoni, Humanity Literacy provides the common ground and foundation for this frame of reverence. We draw upon each student's innate ability to speak with anyone, as if they were coming from the same place or were part of the same family, simply because they can love more. Students creatively think up similes, analogies, and metaphors that are globally current and comprehensible, yet still have the resonance of the speaker's unique personality. Humanity Literacy is not a course in cliches, but, rather, illuminates a way of relating with people which allows the ever-present mutual interest, respect, and love to break free from conventions, and to broaden and deepen our repertoire of relationship.

The purpose of Humanity Literacy is to provide the essential package of knowledge, including concepts, terms, pictures, and diagrams, such that each possessor of this awareness will be able to venture forth and communicate as a potential friend to virtually everyone. A common view, even if it initially seems tentative or tenuous, can be the seed of a trusting, growing relationship with any other person on the planet, irrespective of age, nationality, religious faith, creed, color or other semantic segregation. Humanity Literacy is a whole bag of these seeds; Nizhoni is the fertile garden, and the conscious awareness of the students provides the light, warmth, and nourishment for growth.

Humanity Literacy focuses on five things that humans all have vitally in common, and like to talk about: Health, Wealth, Wisdom, Energy, and Destiny. Each topic is the tip of an information iceberg. As individuals, we can readily see the small fraction that has to do with us personally, which bobs above "see-level." Our knowledge of our own bodies and possessions, for instance, is so obvious to us that it almost eclipses the vast majority of what would be important to us, were we only conscious of our larger Selves as aspects of Humanity.

If we could consistently pay attention to larger aggregates of awareness, we would be cognizant of the whole information iceberg, and grow more whole ourselves. The very structure of Humanity Literacy is based on the Levels of Succession: Body, Family, Company, Community, Society and Humanity. By using ourselves as the starting points, we seek to build a sense of personal urgency and immediacy not found elsewhere. By moving up methodically from one natural grouping to the next, we maintain our perspective, our sense of balance. For example, in addition to our own health, we are affected by the health of our families, companies, communities, societies, and Humanity itself. Thus, when we talk about "my health" at Nizhoni, we really mean "our health", to the extent that we can stretch our own awareness to encompass others.

The alternative, to focus from the start on the entire world, or even on *Gaia*, the living planet, is to risk spinning our youth into the ranks of the Cassandras, who can see catastrophes on the horizon, but are emotionally overwhelmed and feel powerless to take personal, constructive, and immediate action. In one survey, several dozen teens were asked about the future and about half reportedly said there wouldn't be one. This nihilism is all we can expect from the psychologically crippled possessors of Humanity Illiteracy. Saying "People (or politicians or multinationals or Generals) are killing the planet. I am helpless before this terrible strain of idiots running things," is self-indulgent and may be a step toward alienation, misanthropy, and even mental illness.

A Humanly Literate person would start with herself, and first ask whether she was living in a wholly healthy manner, and then, with the speed of thought, look at her influence for good or ill at each Level of Succession. She might conclude by saying, "I am sponsoring the eutrophication (algae clogging) of our fresh water with my laundry soap, and don't really want to trade sparkling lakes for sparkling plates. I will stop, and extend my influence into the other groups of which I am a constituent." Other problems might be assessed by going down the Levels of Recursion from Humanity to Society and so on down to you, or me, without blame or boast.

Humanity Literacy is about the ascension of awareness and the explosive expansion of the idea of the self. Alternatively, it is about the miniaturization and personalization of planet-sized phenomena. It creatively articulates a vocabulary that properly explains and models our common, interdependent identity as global awareness itself. Thus, students become teachers on the first day, and they continue from there, bringing coherence and meaning with each meeting, recognizing that they are a Collective Consciousness together, and that any increase in awareness, intelligence, or consciousness for one, aids and enables us all.

As the five topics above might have indicated, Humanity Literacy includes five core courses, each of which provides a context in which students can see the parts they play in the whole, in the physical hologram we call "Earth", from body to Humanity. The courses are:

Terra Sapiens: Healing the Body of Humanity

Earth, Inc.: Enriching the Company of Humanity

The Information Foundation: Upgrading the Mentality of Humanity

Human Fusion: Merging the Entities of Humanity

Cogenesis: Manifesting the Destiny of Humanity

Each of these courses is a book in itself, as is **Humanity Literacy: A Guide to Global Awareness**. Knowledge can be compressed and compacted onto the printed page, but only so far. These books, now in preparation, attempt to sketch out the context and direction of relationship, but *living* the awareness is what truly matters. This chapter provides only an introductory glimpse into the subject matter, serving the role that an appetizer does for a feast with friends. By using examples from Terra

Sapiens and other courses, a sense of the integral themes that give the course its value and coherence can be introduced. To get the full story, though, come to Nizhoni!

A fundamental principle of Humanity Literacy, to paraphrase the foregoing, is that you start with your body in developing a frame of reverence. You need to start with yourself because, of course, it incorporates that which is most relevant, inspiring and motivating to you. Your own body is a great laboratory, where you will be able to try the concepts and processes suggested in the course. You can directly experience how your actions work to actually change your being and awareness of the levels of succession, and do this without depending on anyone else, achieving immediate effect.

We start with the body as a system, focusing more on process than on static description. In *Terra Sapiens* we talk about a healthy body as being one that is whole and in balance, in dynamic equilibrium. This involves adaptation and evolution and other processes which allow the organism both to change his/her/its environment and/or adapt to it. When we are in the state and process of dynamic equilibrium, all forces that work to push us off center just cancel each other out, leaving us poised for accomplishment. We discuss the nineteen subsystems of the body and the maintenance of health, both individually and collectively. Biology and chemistry, mathematics and art, and other useful high school lessons are covered, not as texts to mentally copy, but as Maps of the Self. And then we discuss the relevance and applicability of these concepts as we intellectually ascend to family, to school or company, to the community, to society, and to Humanity as a whole, remaining consistent with the metaphor of healing our collective body.

We go through these levels of succession methodically to help students gain confidence through staged completions of comprehension. We gift them with a mental tool kit to grasp vast, complex systems, using the Levels like a manual transmission, shifting gears from neutral to first and so on. We guide students to overcoming feelings of being overwhelmed and dropping back—or dropping out—when they do not understand or if they fail to see immediate results. This lesson relates to leadership: we want Nizhoni students to realize that they can accomplish great things, but that great things usually take a great deal of time, and result from a great number of smaller efforts. Focusing energy for the long haul is not something teenagers usually do naturally. But the students here at Nizhoni have come to ride the Long Wave, not just the roller coaster. The greater the Level of Succession, the more energy and time—and patience—we must each put in to have observable effect.

After providing a sense of what health is for individuals in dynamic equilibrium, through diet, exercise, mindful attention, and freedom from addictions, among other factors, we study how to measure and improve the health of each student's family. It is important for students to be able to develop and apply their own metrics to their families, thinking for themselves while still being open to the insights of other students. We encourage students to actually, not just hypothetically, involve their parents. Fathers and mothers have come to Humanity Literacy classes and participated, often to the students' joy or mock dismay. This has the effect of bringing the lessons to life, and retaining the new knowledge in the form of new family practices and in-jokes.

With this personal and family anchoring, we then bring the focus up to the School itself, asking students how to maintain or improve the health of Nizhoni and its constituents, be they students, faculty, their families, visitors, or suppliers. Students come up with their own responses to the question: how do we incorporate each person's needs, desires, and special gifts, while maintaining wholeness, perfection, and balance? And, once students develop an answer that they can live with, they act accordingly, striving to practice what they seek to preach.

Out of these discussions, Nizhoni is constantly and consciously renewed and revitalized. Students feel that they are co-creators, and not just consumers, of their School. At this point we talk about our transition from educators to entrepreneurs, and how schools differ from companies. The students develop an awareness that not all enterprises and industries are equally conducive to good physical and mental health while, alternatively, they learn that they often have very inaccurate notions of actual business practices.

In one class discussion on careers with companies, the students practically mutinied, with over half stating they wanted to be healers, not business people. A guest speaker, who happened to own four hospitals, then pointed out that he shared their desire to heal. As a "healer," he could help several people that day, but as a "businessman," he was helping—albeit indirectly—several hundred people and could, additionally, cope with a far greater diversity of maladies via the instrument of his enterprises. Our students got the point, but what about the three billion or so other young people to whom comes the inheritance of the approximately hundred million enterprises of this earth? If we expect them to pay for the debts of their fathers, we need to better communicate the benefits of incorporated effort.

With this understanding, the class focuses its now-significant expertise on the health of communities, and then on that of our diverse societies in American, West Germany, the European Community, and beyond. For example, students may discuss whether New Zealand or Tahiti, its neighbor across the South Pacific, is healthier. Initially, some may regurgitate travel slogans from TV in support of the healing effects of Polynesian sunshine. After some investigation, though, they learn more about the quiet Kiwi county, with its nuclear-free islands, comprehensive health care and education, and freedom from foreign military forces or control, and also about Tahiti's nuclear testing and dumping. For all its alluring attributes at the level of the body, Tahiti has characteristics of a laboratory and a dump at the larger levels. Through such discussions, students come to learn, not only the facts behind the facades, but also how good citizens have tried to heal their countries. They gain the enlarged understanding that leads to greater ability to be responsible.

And then we come to healing Humanity, and our Earth, which Time Magazine called "Planet of the Year," in place of "Man/Woman of the Year," This undertaking, after they have thoroughly learned to apply a healing methodology at each of the other levels of succession, is straightforward and natural for the students. They go through a four-phase process: Observation, Diagnosis, Prognosis, and Prescription. As with each of the other levels, they identify health-impairing situations, they make predictions about what will happen if the current course is continued, and then they recommend holistic, systematic solutions and implementation plans, eventually including schedules, budgets, and success metrics.

At the planetary level, the students are pleased and surprised to find that the Earth itself performs this process of maintaining its own dynamic equilibrium. For example, the Earth has maintained a constant temperature over the centuries, even with tremendous fluctuations in solar radiation. The Earth has constantly maintained the salinity of the oceans at 3.4 percent, even though salt is always rushing in from land deposits. This is significant because beyond this salinity level, life is threatened: at 6 percent salinity, cell walls disintegrate. If the Earth had not maintained this balance, and salt concentration had increased, all life in the ocean—which at one time included all life—would have been terminated. Students learn about Lovelock's Gaia hypothesis of the living Earth, and often become thrilled by the ideas that start popping up, and the connections that start taking place between the great and small.

Nizhoni students relate bodily to this knowledge, given both the expansion of successive revelation, and their personal involvement every step of the way. They start to sense the planet as alive, its temperatures as the climates, its blood as the waters, its breath as the winds.

From a physical identification with the entire Earth itself come the sparks of the student's own global identity. These sparks are fanned by the Nizhoni community into flames which burn away the superfluous, tenuous, and selfish, leaving only the essential, eternal, and selfless sense of global consciousness.

The concept of dynamic equilibrium weaves its way through the whole of Humanity Literacy. As an ideal, it causes students to seek point and counterpoint, to look at multiple sides of an issue. Further, it inspires the more advanced students to engage in the dance of the dialectic with each other and by themselves, using the twin tools of solitude and multitude. They find or create a thesis, collide

and compare it with its antithesis and bring forth
a new synthesis. In this environment, neither students nor teachers become limited by language,
constrained by culture, or devoted to their dogmas.
We keep our minds open and our hearts full
enough to share.

Nizhoni is educating women and men to become
Cultural Engineers who will create the themes,
archetypes, and other cerebral signatures on the
parchment of the public mind. They will create
memes, or units of cultural inheritance that are the
informational counterpart to genes, the units of
genetic inheritance. All their lives, students have
unwittingly consumed the memes of Public Rela-
tions, Advertising, and Propaganda: society's
PRAP. These memes programmatically colonize,
pollute, and lay waste to young minds. Now, they
will be able to clear the PRAP out, perform "information inoculations," for themselves and others,
and then start to put their own "fact factories," into
production. In effect, students can then grow their
own "meme ecosystem," for a more healthy and
adaptable ecology of consciousness.

The Nizhoni meme makers are not constrained
by one country's view of the world or one language's way of condensing, limiting, and filtering
the world out for its own purposes. Though English is the language of instruction at Nizhoni, we
constantly extend it with words from other
tongues, building a Tower of Babel by design,
where each student begins with the common
tongue, and then adds words and memes from his

or her own language, and others. Nizhoni attracts well-travelled students from many countries, most of whom speak two or more languages, some of whom speak four or more tongues. Adding to this melting pot of memes gives additional satisfaction to the students as they build the culture of the school: use of "your" word provides a pulse of pleasure whenever you hear it. This linguistic sensitivity leads each Nizhoni person to be seen as both polite and cosmopolite in his or her travels.

Our experience with the Nizhoni community gives us growing confidence that a common world language can be brought forth. The *Terran* or *Gaian* language won't be like Esperanto or other contrived languages, but rather will be a simplified English that borrows heavily from the "East," especially Japanese, Russian, Chinese, and Arabic; and continues to absorb from the rest of the "West," including German, Spanish, French, and Italian. In addition, certain tribal or native words of power and uncommon sensitivity will come into common use. The Navaho word for "beauty-way", Nizhoni, is my favorite. "Aloha", which indicates well-wishing at both greeting and parting is similar. It actually means "the way of peace." Our growing language returns to the roots of social memory, the tribal mind, and resumes integral use of symbols, diagrams, and pictures to convey meaning, in addition to Eastern, Western, and Native words.

A saying attributed to Confucius has it that a picture is worth 1,000 words. In a computer, 1,000 words takes up about 10 kilobytes of memory, as does a simple, small picture. This not only provides modern support for ancient wisdom but, more importantly, shows us that we can use new tools to widen the band-width of communication, and substitute colorful illustration for tedious translation and interpretation. A photograph-quality color picture can be "worth"—or equivalent in memory—to ten thousand or more words. Digitized pictures can be saved, stored, or retrieved upon demand with a single keystroke, each on a computer, but with thousands of times the information content of that keystroke. When Nizhoni students write papers, they illustrate them, using magazine clippings and bit-mapped graphic art stored on computers. The emphasis is on communication, rather than just highly-programmed replication, and the band-width is wide open.

The result is papers that are almost works of art, interesting, expressive, personal, and a joy to read and view. Selected papers, in turn, are transformed further into videos and plays, inspiring these artists of expression to think holographically, or wholly in pictures. As humans, we think naturally of three dimensions, in color, and with motion. Regrettably, most books and computer screens are two-dimensional, monochrome, and without animation. This information-poor presentation modality takes its mental toll, and may even make habitual observers less intelligent by inducing their senses to atrophy. Language is a vehicle, and Nizhoni's people use whatever it takes to go farther and faster in the race to relate. Each learns to be unconstrained by prior conceptualization or mode of presentation.

Students consciously apprehend complex themes and memes via visual metaphors. For "dynamic equilibrium," the class imagines a person walking on a tightrope, carrying many things with him. When he is in balance, it means that all these different forces that are around him are cancelling each other out and he is in an effortless state of grace, balanced without force of will or tension. Yet, let him get a little bit off of this imaginary, non-dimensional point of balance, and he finds it very hard to regain equilibrium. With this metaphor presented once, students can reflect behavior out of balance with great clarity, and perhaps hilarity, simply by wobbling.

Mentally or kinesthetically (bodily), sensing one's center of gravity and maintaining balance during change is a skill applied throughout the course. The levels of succession can be seen as concentric circles. You start with yourself, and, with constant awareness that you are a **Center of Influence**, you mentally radiate out in a quantum step to perceptually encompass a larger circumscribing ring, which represents the people close to you, your family, and then you see or feel yourself successfully applying relevant concepts there, and then you radiate further to your company and so on, always retaining a comfortable central position as the **agent of convergence**.

All of the foregoing, including the levels of succession. metaphors, and primacy of personal responsibility, are extensions of the meaning behind the title: *Terra Sapiens: Healing the Body of Humanity.* We humans are cells in the body of Humanity. We have 50 to 60 trillion cells in our body that join to form a metropolis of cells, each of which has a life of its own. If a single cell is sliced off and put alone under a microscope, it may initially seem to be stunned, but then awaken and seek food, like a small amoeba. Each human can be seen to be one of over five billion cells in the Body of Humanity, with consequent responsibility for the healing of the Whole.

The force of evolution, according to some, guides certain organisms and organizations to rise to higher and higher levels of complexity via the successful utilization of higher orders of information. Apprehended information can often negate and even reverse the force of entropy which moves systems from a higher state of order to a lower state. By taking systems to a higher level of order rather than a lower one, certain quanta of information apparently repeal the Second Law of Thermodynamics, which defines entropic degradation. At Nizhoni, we are providing a higher order of information to students and preparing them to utilize it for their own growth. Cells we may be, but some cells, like brain cells, must specialize and integrate to take responsibility for the viability of the whole. Teenagers are like undifferentiated cells in the womb of society before they have chosen their mates and careers. Nizhoni makes it possible for them to see and succeed beyond what is obvious to their brother cells, and to specialize and collaborate to take responsibility for the whole of Humanity.

With knowledge comes power and, with power, responsibility. What should we do with this body? We should heal it, because we are only healthy when everybody in Humanity is healthy. Given that we breathe in air that other people breathe out, eat food that grows from soil in which we bury our dead, and bathe in water we pour our wastes in, *there is no boundary* between each of us and all of us where the streams of inputs and outputs do not mix and change. We are all part of the same circulating fluids of life, pumped by the pulse of Earth, for better or worse.

Terra Sapiens is our name for a state of integrated human evolution, in which all our diversity sums up into a great Unity. Terra Sapiens is a model, an illustrative concept, a metaphor presented to change the students' perspectives, as are each of the five title concepts. Why use these hyper-real concepts? Because Humanity Literacy requires a constant expansion of consciousness as far above the disconnected facts accepted as knowledge as the students can comprehend. The course titles induce and accelerate this shift.

Still, the word is not the thing: no matter how many descriptive terms one lists, the living being will still be greater than the sum of these terms. We are not just collectives of facts, despite the best efforts of some outdated educators to make it seem so, in order to use scripts in which to compare scribbles and from which to pass judgment on individual worth and potential. Every system that aims to educate or draw forth the best in people must have comprehensive coherence, from which it follows that each Nizhoni course, and even each constituent presentation, focuses on a topic which within itself contains the whole. Health is about wholeness, and the Nizhoni kids receive it wholeheartedly as such.

Health is essential, but there is more to life, and to Humanity Literacy, than just health. An understanding of **Wealth**, by which we mean "the relative ability to be, do, and have whatever you seek that considers the greater good", is also important. The second course is about Wealth and is called *Earth, Incorporated: Enriching the Company of Humanity*. The metaphor in this case is that we are all owners, operators, and employees of the greatest company in the world: Earth, Incorporated. The point is that we all must work together, and that each of us can become truly and sustainably rich only if we assist other people in becoming wealthy as well. And in this course we talk about entrepreneurship, global advertising and marketing, and fundamentals of business practice such as finance and markets, hierarchies and networks.

Students also gain the systems perspective and learn the fundamentals of Operations Research and Cybernetics, the science of effective organization. Cybernetics shows how viable systems, those that can maintain an independent identity, are organized. Students see clearly the five related systems that all organisms and organizations have in common, and learn about the transformative effects of positive and negative feedback. And Operations Research, which provides a methodology for solving complex problems with teams of experts from different fields, gives students an uncommon ability to take on and complete adult-level tasks. This is an important aspect of our program because Nizhoni staff seek out challenging internships from which the students will earn both recognition and remuneration.

The first course deals with how to remain viable and in optimum health. The second course takes health as a given, relating how to develop options and choices for constructive courses of action, and build teams and enterprises to accomplish substantive tasks. Still, balance between health and wealth is stressed to temper future student temptations to profit at the expense of people. The Korean people could perhaps have benefited from this sense of ethics: the South Korean who earned the most money in 1987 was the female president of the company which holds the monopoly on tear gas production. She "earned" $7.3 million, while the Korean people sampled her wares.

The third course, on *Wisdom*, deals with complex questions of morality, ethics, and intelligence when faced with choices. Students learn to ask, "Once I have all my options, how do I sense which is best for me." And which is best for us all? We begin this course, which is entitled *The Information Foundation: Upgrading the Mentality of Humanity*, with a look inside our own mind, and progress to the concept that each of us is an aspect of a great, Global Mind. The mind is not just the brain, and a great mind, like that of Socrates or Gautama the Buddha, lives on long after the brain is gone. The mentality of Humanity refers to the rich, thriving interaction of all the thoughts we have together. We complement each other so well, with many wonderfully varied views of everything humanly conceivable. This common mentality of Humanity is our greatest gift, but is not without shortcomings. For one thing, we collectively retain "knowledge" that is obviously false or counterproductive, or see life through warped reality-tunnels. There is nothing more dangerous than an obsolete idea that refuses to die. Thankfully, the truly great ideas, like love and peace, never die. They just get lost or warped in cluttered minds.

In this course, we enable students to see themselves as programmers of "social software," which is nothing less than the grand sum of all "code-able conduct." We run our lives, families, companies, and so on, according to innumerable rules which proscribe what is appropriate or mandatory according to a given system. We emulate biocomputers given dozens of often incompatible sets of obsolete, even conflicting programs. Every action we take, individually or collectively, writes more code that directs the course of human conduct. The new social contract dictates that we fix these invisible errors: Coder, Debug Thyself.

At Nizhoni, we cultivate the masterful detachment of a skilled programmer, who follows a simple methodology for systems development: define, design, develop, deploy and debug. Debugging is the process of testing to see that the software does exactly what it was intended to do. If it does not work or does not compute, then the programmer or coder will isolate the problem area, change a few things, test it, and keep changing code until the program works as desired or specified. At Nizhoni, we train our programmers of social software to identify habits, policies, and even laws that just do not work as desired or promised, and to propose and personally or collectively implement workable solutions. They work to debug the glitches in life.

In this course, students receive unique insights into the optimal use of computers, as well as awareness of the useful applications and related limitations to applying the digital systems paradigm to people. Input, processing, and output, are a simple starting point for people, who have roughly analogous processes: they sense, cogitate (think and feel), and relate to what they sense. With this simple model of cognition, along with dozens of other maps of the Mind, we have a template for our efforts to increase the holographic awareness, intelligence and consciousness of teachers and students, starting with how we *sense*.

We humans have this odd notion that we can utilize only five senses—six, if we are paranormal. During this course at Nizhoni, we talk about over 70 distinct senses that are exhibited by certain humans and other members of the animal kingdom, including temperature, pressure, navigation, radiation, electricity, tone, and so on. In the class, the students are taught that they can, with proper, focused application, develop amd emulate to some extent the senses of any creature, great or small. This work is complemented by the world-class instruction students receive in communicating with animals, which spans the spectrum from relaxing tense rats (by rubbing their tiny ears) to healing sore horses. We go through meditations and guided exercises to focus awareness on these other, often never before used senses. Like tourists with many cameras, students open new apertures to their world and record their impressions with greater precision. Once they open wide these unused portals to experience, students can recreate the world.

We explore how we *feel*, and how our emotions affect us, viewed through the hologram of the Emotional Body. All of our genes combine to form our genome. Conceptually parallel to the genome is the Emotional Body, the sum of all of our intense feelings. The Light Institute experience in healing thousands of emotional bodies over the years is provided uniquely to Nizhoni, and some students come to the School as a result of the profoundly positive effect the work has had on a family member or other loved one. All students do the Light Institute work in their first week. Typically, the students will emerge with several intimately relevant and meaningful life experiencs, to which they will refer for insight repeatedly to move through their deepest challenges.

We have found that the work of the Light Institute is highly conducive to the rapid personal growth of Nizhoni students. Though it occupies only a small fraction of the student's total academic year, the work sets the School apart from all others. Through the work, we acknowledge that each student is already a very wise being, one who can access lifetimes of valuable experience for constructive purposes. The work enables students to have a vivid and very personal experience of themselves as great beings, and call henceforth on their own unlimited Higher Self for guidance. This engenders self-confidence, self-love, and self-sufficiency. The students feel so full of experience, love, and time that their *angst*, or anxiety, about competing or fitting in dissolves, and they are emotionally available to share with others. And this all strengthens the rest of Humanity Literacy.

With emotional bodies cleared, we explored how we *think* and cover the many different aspects of intelligence, such as verbal, spatial, and logical. We go through exercises to develop the holographic capacities of the brain, and provide new accelerated learning tools and techniques for the students to use.

Students then practice new modes of *relating*. We indicate ways that students and teachers can broaden their repertoires of relationship so that each and all can put these many heightened senses, balanced emotions, and increased multiple intelligence to use for the benefit of others.

This leads us nicely toward *Energy*, the fourth course: *Human Fusion: Merging the Entities of Humanity*. In the third course, we relate how to choose the "smartest" course of action, determine one's purpose, and develop vast personal capabilities toward fulfillment of that purpose. But all truly great purposes involve some degree of collaboration with other people. In *Human Fusion*, we go further, and cause students to ask, "Now that I have my purpose, how do I get others to join with me to accomplish my highest aims?" and, "How do I merge all these different levels we have talked about?" This leads us to adopt other metaphors. In addition to being a body, and part of a company or mentality, we can be part of or influenced by many different entities that do not fit neatly or concentrically together.

Human Fusion deals with the great need to merge the many groupings of awareness people have as a result of systems of thought such as religions, philosophies, politics, professions, and so forth. The challenge for each student is to help make an environment which is rich enough, hot enough, to make different groups of people flow together—in effect, melting and merging. Franklin D. Roosevelt and the Melting Pot live again, only the human stew is much more varied and delicious!

In this course we make the distinction between **fission**, which unleashes tremendous energy in often uncontrolled, unmanageable, and ultimately destructive manner, and **fusion**, which unleashes less energy, and that only within a very hot, controlled environment, but with the compensating benefit of sustainability and reduction in humanly-harmful radioactivity. Fusion is the process of coming together and making one out of two or more, with a consequent greater capacity to perform useful work. This course, *Human Fusion*, explains how people have created social super-organisms throughout history, often through religion. We discuss seven great religions (Hinduism, Buddhism, Taoism, Confucianism, Islam, Judaism, and Christianity), with an emphasis on the spectrum of attraction these have articulated to consistently draw people together for centuries for a range of purposeful actions. We then draw upon this background to discuss the relevancy of these religions to events or happenings, such as killing a writer, or being a martyr on behalf of the order, and how to live peacefully yet boldly in such a world.

The students interact in discussions relative to the potential for drawing on selected aspects of each religion to form an integrated system of reverence, one which respects all faiths to some extent, without totally rejecting the others. Once developed, this sacral knowledge may be shared and shifted through apprenticeships. In societies with a climate of increasing fundamentalism and mutual intolerance, this simple attempt to seek out the common benevolent themes and develop a spiritual synthesis may prove useful, once warring parties have exhausted themselves and find exploration of alternatives preferable to continued battle. Our "fundamentalism" at Nizhoni deals with the education of the soul, and the healing of the emotional body. By delving into the bonding power of the great faiths, students can understand and transcend old social constraints on their growth in consciousness. They know the truth—that all religions have value, and that no one has a monopoly on God—and the truth sets us free.

In the final course, we work with *Cogenesis: Manifesting the Destiny of Humanity*, wherein each student is given the opportunity to articulate how s.he would guide our common future. In this class, the students (and, often, parents) do nearly all the talking and teaching. Somehow, the class always seems to end up talking about what the students love, and about their desire to let everyone take, and make, more love.

Together, these five courses make up Humanity Literacy and articulate much of the Nizhoni philosophy of Earth-sized awareness. It is worth mentioning three aspects of global consciousness at Nizhoni. First, students come from many countries around the world, making the school itself a multi-national institution. Second, most students are very well-traveled. At dinner, one may hear conversations such as a discussion of comparisons of, say, Bombay with Basel and Boston. Third, our students are invariably highly interested in planetary challenges. They have a desire to make a contribution on a global level. All told, these factors make a program like Humanity Literacy become food and fuel for global consciousness.

We work very hard on the fundamentals, on the terms and concepts that capable college-bound students are expected to know. We are able to add all the new and unique material for a simple reason: unlike most other schools, which chop up subjects into one-hour blocks, we deal with topics through areas of convergence which reinforce the learning process—a far better method than the usual one of commencing a class session reminding (bored) students of previous learning.

At Nizhoni, reminding is rarely necessary because we build rapidly upon the last set of knowledge presented, and provide information that can be used to make meaningful contributions immediately and personally. At the end of each class, each day, the students have achieved a whole new level of comprehensive understanding, rather than having merely logged a series of data sets which they will subsequently need to determine how to assimilate.

We are enhancing the program by adding three *Senses* sessions because the students enjoy those parts of the course where they perceived the manner in which "everything" spoken of is integrated and becomes coherent, and the complexity is seen as an aspect of the subject's beauty. We start with a one-week program called *Sense of Self*, in which we explore all the ways and means by which a student can know who s.he is in the world. The answer to the question of "Who are you, and how do you know?" changes for each considerably from beginning to end. Exercises to develop each of the students' seventy senses are performed by the group, so that each can practice whenever s.he feels a need to develop and enhance a given sense.

We then go to the semester program and five days of instruction per week. Each day we deal with one of the courses: *Health* on Monday, *Wealth* on Tuesday, *Wisdom* on Wednesday, *Energy* on Thursday, and *Destiny* on Friday. Each of these is taught, to the extent possible, as a whole, with one to three major themes each day. In the middle of the class year, just before the Winter Holiday, we have the second sense class, *Sense of Convergence*. Here we draw all the courses together, attempting to make the complex comprehensible and the intangible graspable. Here we talk about how to conceptually encompass the whole, even though parts or factual fragments are apparently unrelated.

In *Sense of Convergence*, we relate to students, among other things, three major concepts: **connectivity**, how to connect oneself strongly with large numbers of people and information instruments; **inter-operability**, how to exchange information in order to do useful cooperative work; and **adaptability**, how to organize in such a way that the original benefits of these groups are retained as they grow, by setting up systems that promote multiple uses by multiple users. With these concepts, we teach students to build systems that engender convergence. In addition, we present examples of chaos or entrophy, and talk about how to avoid being arrested by Murphy's Law—Anything that can go wrong, will!

In the second half of the year we change formats from lectures and discussions to workshops. In a simple way, we try to emulate the teaching technique usually credited to the Harvard Business School, the Case Study Method. We start with a case (a report on a challenging situation or a complex problem of 10 to 20 pages) and work through the case by calling on students to provide their insights. As an example for *Health*, we talk about how people working for WHO, the World Health Organization, wiped smallpox from the face of the earth, after the disease had caused centuries of pain and disfigurement. WHO's problem was, how do you make sure that everyone who needs a vaccination receives it? Students are asked to propose solutions, and are then—their interest whetted by the challenge—provided with a detailed description of WHO's successful approach, which was that, upon hearing reports of smallpox, WHO personnel would pinpoint the incident on a map and then draw a circle to scale with a radius of five miles from the incident. Medical teams led by WHO personnel would then vaccinate persons within the indicated area, most of whom resided in villages facing simple roads. Thus, WHO did not at that time attempt to vaccinate every single person on earth (an impossibly difficult task) but, rather, applied the medicine right where it was needed most at the time.

After grasping the strategy and methodology involved in this example, students are offered the opportunity to deal with AIDS, which has been described as a disease of our global culture, and for which the routes of Boeing 747's are vectors (direction and extent of incidence). Actual practitioners in the field comment on summarized student conclusions in many of our classes in order to expand our students' ability to comprehend diverse points of view on the topic they have been given to work with.

For *Wealth*, students become **Enterprise Engineers**. They learn about entrepreneurship and write business plans for companies, going through the process of creating a *Vision*, establishing a coherent *Mission* for the enterprise, choosing an appropriate *Strategy* (with a focus such as low cost, high value, or target market) developing *Tactics* (with schedules, budget, and performance measures) and setting up *Operations* (staffing and plan implementation). This is the way they learn about Research and Development, of turning innovations into products by acting as interdisciplinary operations research teams and playing roles as professionals from diverse fields who much organize to accomplish specified assignments.

Students learn about business administration, becoming managers, executives, marketers, and negotiators, and work under time constraints to enable their chosen enterprises to survive, grow, and earn profits while keeping their moral, ethical, and social responsibilities fulfilled. Cases from the business world will be used to make the point. For example, RJR Nabisco, Inc., was sold to KKR, a New York investment banking firm, for $25 billion. Why did the RJR's Board of Directors reject a higher offer from the current RJR executives and accept what was, in fact, a lower offer from the investment bankers? Was it because the RJR Chief Executive was too greedy after he lowballed his initial bid at $75/ a share, raised later to $112, and gave an overly generous compensation package to himself and a few colleagues? The students come to realize that the Board of Directors based its decision, then, on *non*financial considerations.

Through discussion and renactment of actual cases such as the above, students come to comprehend the importance of integrity, credibility, and rapport in the "real world," and to gain confidence in their ability to establish and maintain productive partnerships and responsible relationships.

For *Wisdom*, students recapitulate the ascension of knowings, from data, to information, to knowledge, to experience, to expertise, to wisdom. They are reminded constantly of the differences between knowledge and wisdom: wisdom is always and only present with consciousness. The wise person is one with a holographic perspective. To get them going up this path, though, we start with the design of information systems and do case studies of organizational use and misuse of information. The executive, legislative, and judicial branches of the United States Government offer ample material for both. Students are asked: "How does the Congress get its information?" "How does this compare with the Japanese legislative information system?" In the Diet in Japan, only a few hundred staff are needed, compared to over 20,000 American Congressional staffers. Does this relate to the fact that the Diet annually passes about 100 out of 120 bills proposed, while the United States Congress introduces over 22,000 bills each term, but passes only a few hundred? Once students reach their conclusions, they come up with suggestions which are sent, as appropriate, to parties that may make use of their insights.

In *Energy*, students develop the capacity for collective action on issues they become concerned about. A student can say, "I care about what I eat. How can I get the companies that process food to stop irradiating food?" The student may do research, try out ideas on classmates, and then say, "I have a plan for Santa Fe. I will talk with these three other groups working on the situation, and see if we can collaborate."

Another student may ask, "How do we promote the planting of our trees?" She will then seek to answer her question with the help of others. We encourage the students to develop their own values, their own commitments, and then to try, to the best of their ability, to inspire other people to work with them, so that they never resort to the "Nobody understands me" escape routine. Nizhoni students know that everyone can understand them and can work with them to do great things. Nizhoni's motto is, *"Think Globally, Act Magnificently."*

In *Destiny*, each week the students map out and articulate what they want to do during next week, month, year, and so on, for many aspects of their lives. Each week they get feedback and see how well they are able to keep on course when they set their own schedules, and orchestrate their own lives. They teach themselves the technologies of time, make the future urgent, and gain an appreciation for eternity.

At the end of each school year, we bring the symphony of lessons to a crescendo, a climax, through a week-long course called *"Sense of Transcendence"* in which students see how they can become greater beings by identifying themselves with their Self first, and carrying that into their family and so on, up the now quite-familiar levels of succession. Each student is shown clearly, via audio and video tapes, how much s.he has grown. What was formerly the ceiling one now finds to be the floor, and, with this reinforcement, the students find themselves feeling whole, balanced, and eager to continue in the academic process next year, after their apprenticeships.

Because Nizhoni is a year-round school students apply these new insights practically. Students will have the opportunity to go on internships to stimulating environments like the Bahamas, the Soviet Union, India, or Brazil. They may go up the Amazon to study deforestation, or down the

Ganges to study desertification. Whenever possible, Nizhoni will obtain consulting assignments for the school so that students can work to solve significant problems, thereby developing a strong sense of self-worth and confidence. In addition, these internships can often produce a set of important case studies for Nizhoni.

Our general schedule is two to three months in Galisteo, with intensive study of the next apprenticeship country's language, and then one month in that country, working with locals on the apprenticeship project.

One unique aspect of Nizhoni relates to communication. Each student is required to write, edit, illustrate and publish a book each year, on a subject mutually agreed to by the student and his or her teachers. Desktop publishing systems are made available and students use them for all phases of the writing process. Through this "write of passage" students will again be brought to understand the hologram of their own learning style and process.

And, for a student who has authored and published two or three 200 page books in high school, the university requirement of a 100 page thesis will seem simple and even elementary. More importantly, students will have mastered the ability to teach themselves to be masters of a given subject, and can literally prove their expertise.

As our development campaign progresses, we are working toward the point at which students will be provided with a "wizard environment" to complement their growing worldly awareness, in which they can obtain the information they need via computers connected to on-line data bases and numerous magazine subscriptions, including several in Japanese, Russian, and languages taught at Nizhoni. In addition, students will learn to use new technologies for "information integration", such as hypertext, expert systems, and intelligent trader's workstations.

New Mexico itself is a wizard environment. Since the Manhattan Project and its atomic achievements, the state has been home to a high concentration of sophisticated technology, such as that used by the world-class scientists and other researchers at Los Alamos National Laboratories, Sandia Laboratories, and the Very Large Array of radioastronomy telescopes. To the extent possible, Nizhoni students will visit and interact with these leading researchers and learn about the infinitely small, vast, and complex via these facilities, in addition to the required biology, chemistry and physics. In these studies, we will try to strike a dynamic balance between practical skills and powerful discoveries and insights relating to chaos, energy, entropy, global security, evolving economies, space technology and genetic engineering. As the conclusion of this book will indicate, though, consciousness is our primary focus, and the greatest tools can serve as extensions of and metaphors for awareness.

Humanity Literacy provides a context for all of the above, into which a student of Nizhoni can pull many insights and facts that seem disconnected, so that each can simply say, "Oh, I see, this relates to health; and this relates to energy; or motivating people to go and help me with my task." When faced with the fire hose of potentially useful knowledge available to the aware person, Nizhoni people will know how to drink from it and, being thus refreshed, renew a small part of Humanity.

Beyond Humanity Literacy

Nizhoni strives to emulate certain well-regarded traits from several of the world's finest universities, adapted for spiritually-aware high school students. This provides them with a solid foundation from which to spring into a college education, should they choose to do so. Students up to the age of 20 attend Nizhoni, including a significant fraction of high school graduates. These men and women use the School as a "Protoversity" in which they can try on different courses of study or professions for size and see how they holistically fit.

This aspect of Nizhoni is the missing link for most teenagers: how to manage the transition from high school to university, without taking off to do simple minded work or unstructured travel, and without switching majors several times when the academic 'reality' of a field does not meet hopes and expectations. Nizhoni can provide a meaningful transition, in a similar manner, though more focused on spirituality and life-style, to Armand Hammer's United World College, our Northern

New Mexico neighbor, which provides education for the senior (last) year of high school and the freshman (first) year of university.

From the Massachusetts Institute of Technology we borrow approaches to teaching students how to solve problems, starting with sets of principles and saying, "What do I need to know to take the next step," and building up the mental tool kit through weekly problem sets. We survey the use of traditional engineering (civil, mechanical, electrical, chemical, and aeronautical) and then attempt to map similar symbolic processes onto four new engineering disciplines: Financial, Enterprise, Social, and Cultural. Students also engage in their own research.

We emulate the Harvard practice of engendering rich and varied interactions with all people in the class, each of whom comes to know the others quite well, by working on group projects and, in addition, working on case studies which show how groups accomplish, or fail, in the real world.

We follow the traditional Oxford practice of providing a tutor, who acts as a mentor or sponsor, someone who watches the student along the way and provides advice on how to stay along the path picked out by the student. The mentor intelligently keeps his young charges on track and on purpose.

Nizhoni aims to develop within students a professional approach to international affairs comparable, for younger students, to that of Georgetown University's School of Foreign Service so that they may participate in more conscious diplomacy.

Nizhoni seeks to gradually build a practice in which, like Tokyo University, instructors will not only watch the students and tell them how they are doing inside the school, but will also help them to build and develop contacts outside the school with other organizations which may want to provide employment or academic admission assistance to qualified students. Most students will be college-bound, and Nizhoni staff will contact admissions personnel to assist whenever needed. This practice of networking on behalf of Nizhoni graduates will improve as our reputation, already considerable for a start-up school, extends. We intend to give each student the opportunity to work with leaders on projects of great importance and interest, and prepare students for their future work as career citizens.

The coming Global Society will create avenues for professional achievement that are presently inconceivable to most students and their parents. Many companies are going out of business or are being taken over while others, are emerging from garages and research projects to grow rapidly and change the structure of entire industries. Big companies are also changing. For example, Japan's C. Itoh, a Sogo Shosha, or "general trading company" does over $125 billion in annual revenue in over 140 countries. Itoh does this with only 10,000 employees (compared to General Motors' 700,000 employees for about $105 billion in annual revenues). C. Itoh now seeks people able to help manage its corporate metamorphosis into a "globally integrated enterprise" via new global information and communication infrastructures. Nizhoni students will gain the requisite variety or skill set needed to succeed in tomorrow's enterprises, whether tiny and nimble or vast and powerful, and all others in between, if a business career is what they wish to pursue.

Other organizations are breaking free of old boundaries to make greater contributions to society. Cooperative research efforts, like Europe's ESPRIT, Japan's Fifth Generation ICOT, and America's Strategic Computing Initiative, all struggle to integrate individuals, companies, and different government agencies to achieve "innovation by proclamation." The highly-regarded Santa Fe Institute brings together Nobel prize winners and world-renowned scholars to gain insights into the sciences of complexity which are broadly applicable, from sub-atomic physics to global security.

A new class of non-profit organizations has begun to sponsor a benevolent web of social ventures. The Greeley Foundation for Peace and Justice, for example, sponsors Soviet-American student exchanges, an International Negotiations Network, and conferences for women leaders. Perhaps more important are the new international alliances, like the European Community, now targeted for 1992 and the South Commission, for the so-called "Third World," We begin to see the wonderful possibility that the *Super Powers* will become *Super Partners*, and begin to disarm. This will give citizens of Earth the challenge of reallocating the trillion dollars of annual military expenditures. For all of these stimulating challenges, Nizhoni students will be ready to join in, and eventually take leadership roles.

Humanity Literacy will extend Thomas Jefferson's educational ideal of "A sound mind in a sound body," to *"A sound mind, body, and soul in a sound Humanity."* Throughout Humanity Literacy, we will use examples that students can apply to their own balanced lives.

With this sense of wholeness and accomplishment, grounded in the soul level and emanating outwards, comes a confidence and a peace, a sense of meaning, which will enable our students to go beyond fear, even fear of death. And, what is more, global consciousness, which may seem quite idealistic now, will actually be seen to be timely, practical, and just the beginning as we go to cosmic consciousness and beyond.

As an example, consider the implications of the work of Albert Einstein, including the Atomic Bomb. His awareness, intelligence, and consciousness changed the course of history. Consider also this story. Else Einstein, his wife, was visiting an advanced observatory in Los Angeles. She listened to a long lecture about the tens of millions of dollars that had gone into designing, building, and operating the facility, filled as it was with optical, electrical, and mechanical systems.

At one point she asked, "But what do you actually do with all this?" Her host replied, "We unravel the complexities of the galaxy, and calculate the course of the cosmos". Mrs. Einstein looked up at the huge telescope, and then around at the complex of machinery, and said, "My husband does that, too, but he just uses the back of an envelope". We aim to enable the families of Nizhoni students to make similar assertions.

One globally-conscious person can change the course of history. The purpose of Nizhoni, when all is said and done, is to spark as many fires and to fuel as many desires to be that person as we possibly can!

* * *

A Personal Message

If you have been inspired by the Nizhoni program you have just experienced, please make a heart-felt motion to contribute to its future, and to that of the world's children. We request that you personally play a part in our success by sending a donation to the Nizhoni School at the address below. We are a nonprofit, tax-exempt organization, making donations tax-deductible.

We also invite you to attend the Nizhoni Venture programs for people of all ages. Please come!

Alex Petofi, Director
Nizhoni:
The School for Global Consciousness
Route 3, Box 50
Galisteo, New Mexico 87540
U S A

Telephone: (505) 982-8293

84754
84754

BP 605 .L53 G752 / Nizhoni

Quimby Library